Exterior Home Repairs

Handyman Club Library™

Handyman Club of America
Minneapolis, Minnesota

Exterior Home Repairs

CREDITS

Tom Carpenter
Creative Director

Mark Johanson
Book Products Development Manager

Dan Cary
Photo Production Coordinator

Chris Marshall
Editorial Coordinator

Jim Barrett, Mark Johanson, Chris Marshall
Writers

Bill Nelson
Series Design, Art Direction and Production

Mark Macemon
Lead Photographer

Ralph Karlen
Photography

Jim Barrett, Dan Cary
Contributing Photographers

John Nadeau
Technical Advisor and Builder

Craig Claeys, Mario Ferro
Contributing Illustrators

ISBN 1-58159-028-8
7 8 9 10 / 06 05 04
© 1998 Handyman Club of America

Handyman Club of America
12301 Whitewater Drive
Minnetonka, Minnesota 55343
www.handymanclub.com

Exterior Home Repairs

Table of Contents

Introduction

Let's face it: there's nothing particularly glamorous or exciting about repairing the exterior of a house. In fact, on most of our lists of favorite handyman activities, caulking windows and patching roofs rank somewhere between washing out the shop vac and sanding wallboard compound. But despite all that, we know enough and care enough about our homes to understand the importance of well-maintained exterior systems. It's these systems that keep us sheltered and dry, shield the interior of the house from exposure to the elements and inform our neighbors exactly what type of homeowners we are. And so, every spring and fall we pull out the extension ladder and venture up to the remotest corners of our roofs, caulk guns in hand, to fix those neverending kinks in the armor of our houses. And despite our grumbling, we're glad we made the effort.

When we put together *Exterior Home Repairs* for our fellow Club Members, it was with two basic questions in mind: *What are the best ways to make these repairs?* and *How can we make the repairs as quickly and easily as possible so we can move on to more interesting projects?*

In striving to answer those questions, we discovered that there's more to making exterior home repairs than simply squirting everything in sight with roof cement or caulk. The major exterior systems are more delicate than we often think, and keeping them in tip-top shape requires a thorough understanding of how they work and a knowledge of which products are best suited for their upkeep. This book is basically the outcome of what we learned about repairing and maintaining roof systems, siding, masonry and foundations, and windows and doors. In each section of the book we've included examples of what to look for when you inspect your house, as well as step-by-step information describing what to do when problems are found. We also try to give you some basic information on how each of the major systems works so you can be better prepared to keep it working well. And finally, we added some material on weatherizing, pestproofing and scheduled home maintenance.

Please take a few moments and review this copy of *Exterior Home Repairs*. We think you'll find it to be packed full of useful information and clear, colorful photographs that show exactly what you need to see. We won't go so far as to promise that reading this book will make you want to jump up out of your chair and replace that missing shingle on your front porch. But we think you'll agree that, with the information in this book, you'll be better prepared for your outdoor chores next spring or fall (or next time the roof starts leaking in the middle of the night or a snowball shatters your kitchen window just as you're sitting down for a holiday meal). And being better prepared helps you get jobs done right, done quickly and done for as little cost as possible.

The exterior of your home

Keeping the exterior of your home in good condition is mostly a matter of understanding how your major house systems work, then conducting regular inspections and performing timely, well-executed repairs. Use this illustration and the maintenance checklists on pages 156 and 157 to help organize your inspections. Refer to the page numbers indicated on the illustration for more information on specific areas of the house.

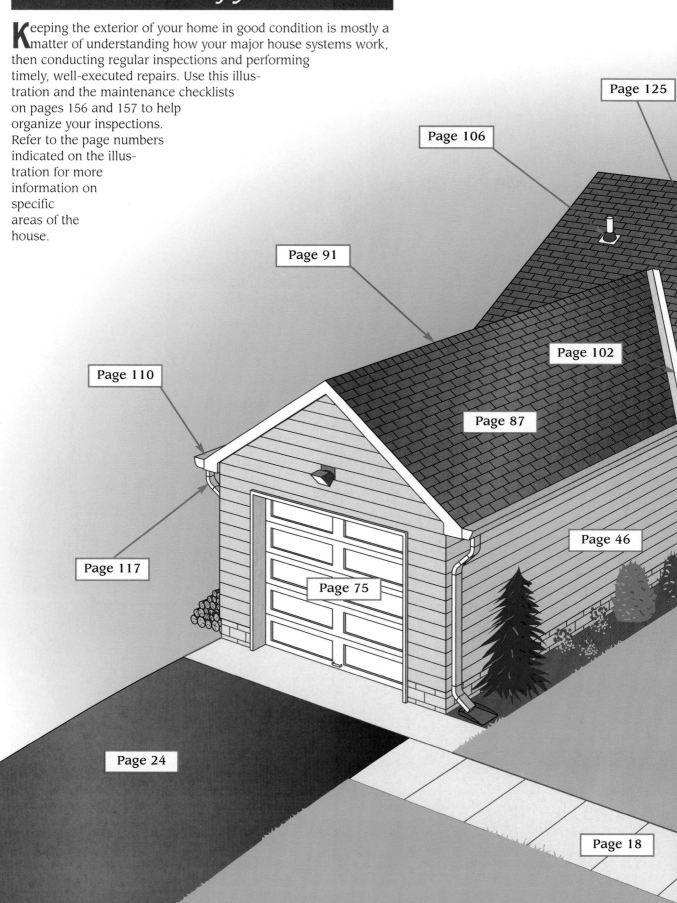

Page 125

Page 106

Page 91

Page 102

Page 110

Page 87

Page 46

Page 117

Page 75

Page 24

Page 18

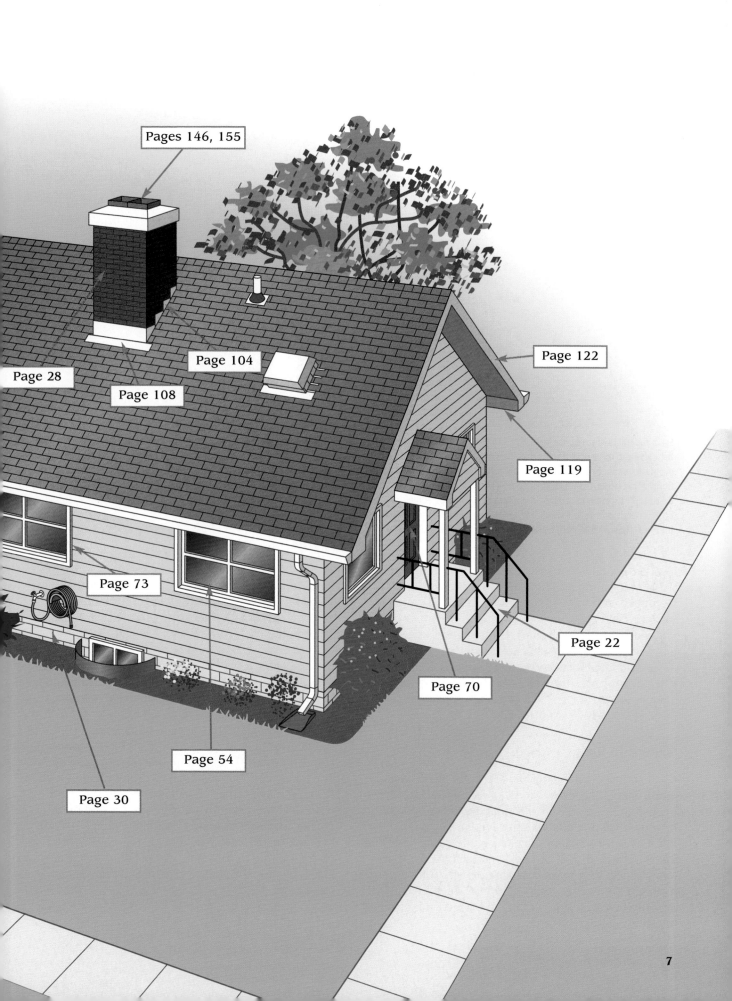

Pages 146, 155

Page 122

Page 104

Page 28

Page 119

Page 108

Page 73

Page 22

Page 54

Page 70

Page 30

7

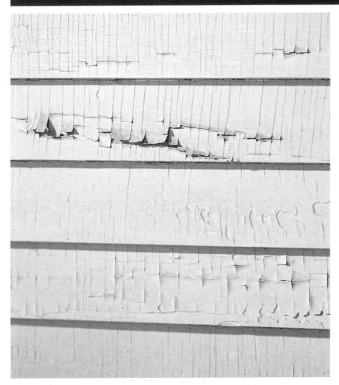

Look for obvious problems first. Peeling paint, crumbling concrete, rotten wood, missing shingles and many of the most common exterior problems announce themselves under even the most casual inspections. More often than not, these problems are caused by other forces that aren't as obvious. For example, the peeled paint above may well be the result of a failed vapor barrier on the interior side of the wall that has allowed moisture build-up to impact the painted surface.

Be on the lookout for signs of moisture problems. Most exterior problems are caused by moisture in some form or another. Mildewed walls, like the one shown above, are a clear indicator that you have a moisture issue that should be dealt with. Other common signs are staining, rotting and general disintegration of any type of surface.

Make scheduled inspections of your home's exterior in the spring and in the fall. Take a systematic approach, starting with the foundation and concrete surfaces and working your way up to the roof systems (or, vice versa if you prefer). Don't forget to check windows, doors, skylights and other openings. In addition to semi-annual inspections, it's also a good idea to check your house for leaks and wind damage after major storms. For detailed seasonal inspection checklists, see pages 156 and 157.

Where to look

First, inspect the house from the outside using binoculars, if necessary, to get a closer look at the roof, including, vents, flashings, chimney, soffits and gutters. If you notice potential damage, venture up to the roof for a closer inspection. Also check the attic, the insides of exterior walls and ceilings, and the basement or crawlspace for signs of moisture penetration or water damage. Don't overlook blistering or peeling paint on exterior surfaces; this is often an early warning sign of moisture problems.

Roofs. Check for loose, missing or damaged shingles. Replace these as soon as you notice the problem to keep the roof weathertight. Inspect flashings around vents, chimneys, dormers and other protrusions through the roof. Also check valley and eave flashings. Look for rust, corrosion and poor caulk seals; renail loose flashings. Look for blockages, such as bird's nests in vents and flues. Check eaves, soffits, fascia and trim for water damage such as rot and peeling paint. Also check for pest damage and blocked soffit vents. Don't overlook trims and flashings at gable ends.

Check gutters and downspouts for loose joints, holes (caused by rust or corrosion), blockages, sagging sections and other damage. Repair promptly to prevent water damage to fascia, soffits and siding.

Inspect the chimney for loose or missing mortar, cracked bricks, cracked or crumbling chimney cap, and leaky or rusted flashings. Most likely, you'll need to get up on the roof to make the inspection. While there, also check the flue for blockages, cracked flue tiles and soot buildup.

Inspect the interior as well. Signs of exterior-related damage are often found on the inside of your home. Ceiling stains like the one above are a good indicator that you may have a leaky roof (although other problems, such as leaky plumbing or inadequate ventilation, may also be the culprit).

Go beyond the surface. Once your quick visual inspection has identified problem areas, probe a little more deeply into the area to determine the extent of the damage. Scrape failed mortar joints or concrete surfaces with a small cold chisel to test the condition of the material surrounding the problem area—sometimes even material that appears to be in good condition is hiding major problems beneath the surface. Also test rotted or spongy wood areas with a screwdriver or awl.

Siding. Check siding for splits, rot, buckling, popped nails and similar damage. Also check for damage caused by termites and other wood-boring insects. Check the condition of the paint. Peeling paint may be due to improper preparation or application, but it can also be a sign of a condensation problem caused by excess moisture inside the house due to poor ventilation or a missing vapor barrier. Check trim for rot, cracks or splits, popped nails and similar damage. Also check for any gaps between the siding and trim, and seal with caulk as needed.

Doors and windows. Check for missing or damaged weatherstripping. Make sure windows and doors operate smoothly and close tightly. Check trim, thresholds and sills for rot and termite damage. Check for damaged or leaky flashings above windows and doors; caulk joints around flashing that need refreshing. Check the condition of window glazing and retainer strips. Replace loose or deteriorated glazing compound and broken or cracked glass. Make sure screens and storm doors/windows fit tightly and are in good overall condition.

Foundations. Start by checking inside the basement or crawlspace for leaks and moisture condensation on interior walls. Find and repair the cause of the problem. Check the foundation from the outside; note any small or large cracks, settling or deterioration. Also inspect for leaks around window wells. Check general drainage conditions; make sure the ground slopes away from the foundation and that water doesn't pool against the foundation after heavy rains. Make sure downspouts carry water well away from the house. Add a downspout extension if necessary.

Walks and driveways. Inspect sidewalks for cracks, spalling, stains, sags and for general surface condition. Check for similar damage to driveways.

Pest damage. Inspect all wood surfaces and adjoining wood structures (porches, stairs, attached decks, fences, etc.) for signs of damage from termites and other wood-boring insects. If you locate these, take immediate action. Inspect all exterior surfaces (roof, siding and foundation) for cracks, holes, gaps, open vents and other potential entry points for insect and rodent pests. Also check inside attics for signs of habitation (birds and rodents).

Making repairs to the outside of your home involves several risk factors that are not typically encountered when working indoors. Wind, rain and sun represent significant safety hazards that must be monitored constantly. Uneven ground and sloping roofs greatly increase the risk of falls. And naturally, any time you're working at heights you increase the chance that a fall will cause serious injury. Other risk factors found outdoors include power lines, the use of long extension cords and the need to work with and transport heavy items like shingles or concrete.

Beyond using plain common sense (probably the most important safety consideration), there are many steps you can take to work more safely outdoors. The information on the following pages provides an overview of good safety information that you'll want to learn and follow. From the work clothes you wear to the type of ladder you use, safety should always be an ongoing concern, whether you're working inside or outside your home.

In addition to following basic rules of personal safety, always be aware of the presence and position of others, especially when working on your roof. Never throw debris or unused materials off the roof without checking for passersby and giving a warning shout. And whenever possible, work with at least one other person in the event an accident should occur.

Proper footwear is a must when performing exterior repairs, especially when working on your roof. Leave your old workboots in the closet if you'll be waking on the roof. A pair of sneakers or soft, crepe-soled shoes will give you much better traction and will be less likely to damage the shingle surfaces.

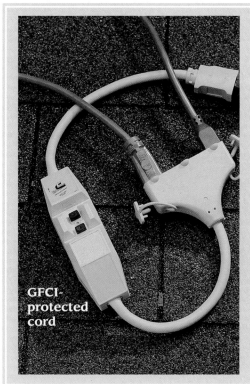

GFCI-protected cord

Working with power

When using power tools outdoors, do not work in damp conditions. Also, make sure tools are plugged into a GFCI-protected outlet. GFCIs (ground-fault circuit interrupters) instantaneously cut off power if the tool or power cord short circuits. Plug-in types are available for unprotected outlets. Or, you can buy a GFCI-protected extension cord like the one shown to the left. Make sure the electrical circuit to be used has enough ampacity to handle the power tools and equipment you'll be using. A 20-amp, 110-volt circuit will handle most portable and stationary power tools. Don't overload circuits by running too many tools at once.

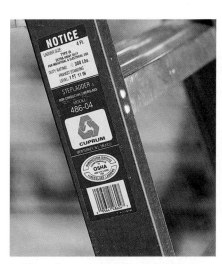

Ladder ratings are printed on labels that are required by law on any new ladder you purchase. Make sure your ladder is designed to support enough load and to be used in exterior conditions. Choose a Type I or Type II class extension ladder. These ratings indicate the safe weight a ladder will bear: 250 lbs. for a Type I ladder; 225 lbs. for Type II; and 200 lbs. for a Type III. The same strength ratings are applied to step ladders.

Safety tips

✔ Set up shop before you start. Store materials so they're convenient to the worksite, yet out of heavy traffic areas. If you need to store materials outdoors, keep a tarp handy in case it rains. Also, keep a wheelbarrow nearby to remove trash from the site as you work—don't allow nails, old shingles and other debris to accumulate on the ground, as they pose a safety hazard. Set up a work table by laying a half-sheet of plywood over a pair of saw horses. Use the table to store tools and other small items off the ground so they don't get wet and are easy to locate.

✔ Keep an eye on the weather. Do not work during stormy weather or in damp conditions. Stay off the roof if it is wet or if the outdoor temperature is too hot or too cold. Do not take on large jobs if you expect a sudden change in the weather.

✔ Dress for the occasion. Basic safety gear includes heavy work gloves for handling materials, rubber gloves when working with cleaners and solvents, eye protection, a respirator or particle mask, full-length pants and long sleeved shirt. When working on the roof, wear knee pads and soft-soled shoes or sneakers. These provide good traction, flexibility and ankle support when working on slopes. Wear a back brace when lifting heavy materials.

✔ When working on the roof, fasten extension cords to the ladder or at the eaves; the weight of a dangling cord can easily pull it (and the tool it's attached to) off the roof. You can buy a fastening device that permanently attaches to a ladder at most hardware stores. Also, pay special attention to the cord location at all times to avoid tripping over it, especially when working off a ladder. A better option is to use cordless tools in high places.

✔ **Stay clear of power lines, electrical service entrances and electrical masts. Use wood or fiberglass ladders instead of metal whenever possible, and fit all ladders with rubber or plastic insulated handles. Do not pressure-wash or hose down surfaces near electrical cables or fixtures.**

Ladder & scaffolding safety

Use a hoist system to transport tools and equipment from the ground to higher places. Never carry heavy loads while moving up and down a ladder. A 5-gallon bucket with an organizer is an excellent vehicle for transporting tools and materials.

A ladder stabilizer connected to the top of your extension ladder improves stability and helps protect the gutters, eaves, siding or roof covering from damage caused by contact from the rails of the ladder.

Ladder & scaffolding safety

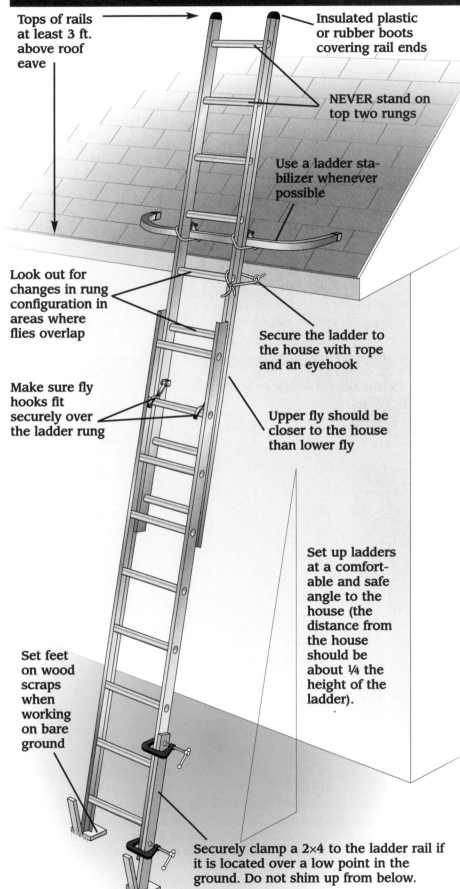

Tops of rails at least 3 ft. above roof eave

Insulated plastic or rubber boots covering rail ends

NEVER stand on top two rungs

Use a ladder stabilizer whenever possible

Look out for changes in rung configuration in areas where flies overlap

Secure the ladder to the house with rope and an eyehook

Make sure fly hooks fit securely over the ladder rung

Upper fly should be closer to the house than lower fly

Set up ladders at a comfortable and safe angle to the house (the distance from the house should be about ¼ the height of the ladder).

Set feet on wood scraps when working on bare ground

Securely clamp a 2×4 to the ladder rail if it is located over a low point in the ground. Do not shim up from below.

Extension ladders are used to make minor repairs at or near the eaves and to access the roof. A sturdy, durable ladder is well worth the extra money you'll pay for it in terms of safety and useful life. Also, choose an extension ladder that will extend at least 3 ft. above the highest eaves on your house. Likewise, step ladders should be tall enough so you don't have to stand on the top two rungs while working. Add a ladder stabilizer or brace at the top end of extension ladders to keep the rails clear of gutters or overhanging shingles and to provide extra stability. Ladder boots keep the rails from marring siding when you lean the ladder against a wall.

Make sure the ladder feet rest on stable ground. In soft ground, slip pieces of plywood or wide blocks

Ladder safety tips

✔ Use both hands when climbing ladders—don't hand-carry tools or materials up a ladder; instead put them in a bucket and hoist up with a rope. When painting, use "S" hooks to hang the paint bucket from a convenient ladder rung.

✔ Have a helper steady the ladder from below as you climb. Keep your hips centered between the ladder rails at all times. When doing jobs while standing on a ladder (such as painting siding or cleaning gutters) don't over-reach. Maintain your balance at all times.

✔ When setting up an extension ladder, make sure both fly hooks are secure and the ladder is at a safe angle. As a rule of thumb, the bottom of the ladder should be one fourth the distance from the wall that the ladder extends up; for example, the bottom of a 20-ft. ladder should be 5 ft. away from the house.

under each ladder foot and drive 1×2 stakes behind the feet to keep them from slipping. On steps or uneven ground, don't shim the "downhill" leg with bricks or blocks. Instead, C-clamp a 2×4 extension to the leg as shown in the illustration on the previous page. You can also buy retrofit kits for aluminum extension ladders that enable you to extend one leg below the other.

Scaffolding provides a broad, stable platform when you need to work at heights for long periods of time or over large areas. You can rent pipe scaffolding from most tool rental companies. Ask for assembly and safe-use instructions. As with ladders, make sure the legs are on stable ground. Most scaffolding has adjustable leg posts to level it on uneven ground. If the scaffold has wheels, make sure they are firmly locked. Trim back overhanging vegetation in the proximity of the scaffolding before you begin to work from it. Disassemble the scaffolding if you will not be using it for an extended period of time—climbing on scaffolding is an inviting (and very dangerous) adventure for young children. Burglars have also been known to gain entry into homes by way of scaffolding.

Additional safety equipment designed for use when working on your roof includes roof brackets and fall arresting gear (See page 86).

One final note: Never use ladders or scaffolding in threatening weather, as these metal structures represent a threat for lightning strikes.

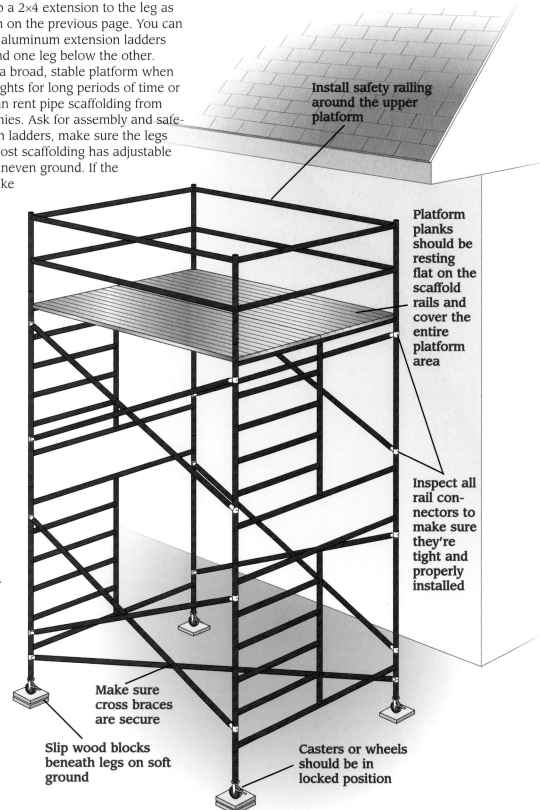

Install safety railing around the upper platform

Platform planks should be resting flat on the scaffold rails and cover the entire platform area

Inspect all rail connectors to make sure they're tight and properly installed

Make sure cross braces are secure

Slip wood blocks beneath legs on soft ground

Casters or wheels should be in locked position

Repairing Masonry & Foundations

Repairing and maintaining masonry walks, driveways, steps and attached patios is an integral part of keeping your home exterior in good shape.

Small cracks, holes and surface defects in walks, driveways and patios are normal and can be repaired easily with various concrete patching products, available at any building center. Large or widespread cracks, sunken or lifted slab sections, and other major structural failures may require you to remove and repour the entire walk, patio or driveway. In new construction, small, isolated cracks may develop within a year or two after a driveway or sidewalk is poured. Causes include initial settling of the subbase and normal expansion and contraction of the base or the slab itself due to seasonal moisture and temperature changes (alternate freezing and thawing, for example). If the slab was installed correctly, the cracks will stabilize and not get any wider.

Because some minor cracking is to be expected, control joints are cut into the slab when it is poured so that when small cracks do develop, they're confined to the joints, making them less noticeable. Larger cracks and holes or widespread cracks are often a result of an unstable base beneath the slab, a slab that is too thin or inadequately reinforced, or an improperly prepared concrete mixture. Surface defects include spalling, crazing, dusting and pop-outs.

Concrete steps have a high exposure to the elements and to stress and are more prone to problems than other types of poured concrete structures. Damaged steps can be rebuilt in some cases, but in most cases the lifespan of steps is shorter than for other structures, and eventually they'll need to be removed and replaced.

Brick and block structures typically develop problems at the mortar joints. As a result, by far the most common repair needed to keep these structures in good condition is tuckpointing the mortar joints.

Concrete repair products

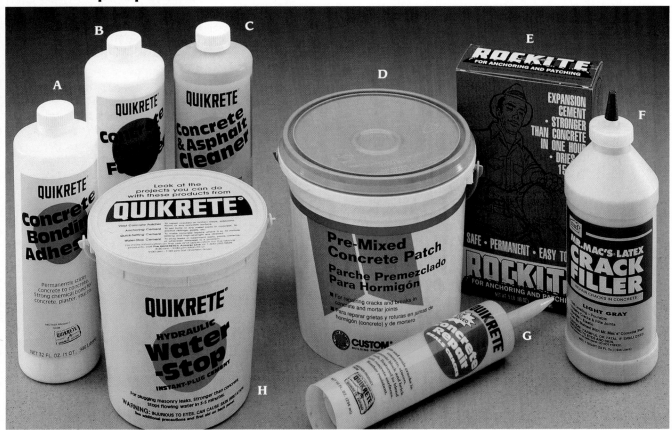

Repair products for masonry and foundations include: **(A) concrete bonding adhesive** to promote better adhesion of concrete repair products; **(B) concrete acrylic fortifier** to increase elasticity of concrete patching material and minimize cracking; **(C) concrete and asphalt cleaner** for regular maintenance and to remove grease and grime that can impair the effectiveness of repairs; **(D, E) concrete patching compound** for filling holes and cracks (pre-mixed and dry powder shown); **(F, G) crack filler** for plugging small concrete cracks up to ½ in. wide in masonry walls or surfaces (liquid and caulk types shown); **(H) hydraulic cement** for patching live leaks.

Concrete repair tools

Repair products for masonry and foundations include:

(A) wood float for smoothing poured concrete; **(B) magnesium float** for smoothing poured concrete to create a hard, slick surface; **(C) mortar hawk** to transport mortar from a mixing vessel to a repair area; **(D) finishing trowel** for smoothing and feathering; **(E) large mason's trowel (London trowel)** for applying mortar in brick and block building projects; **(F) pointing trowel** for applying mortar in smaller repair projects; **(G, H) grooving tools** for finishing and shaping mortar joints (U-shape and V-shape); **(I) edging tool** for shaping edges of poured concrete; **(J) jointing tool** for cutting control joints in fresh concrete; **(K) brickset** for cutting brick and block; **(L, M) cold chisels** (large and small) for chipping and shaping cured concrete.

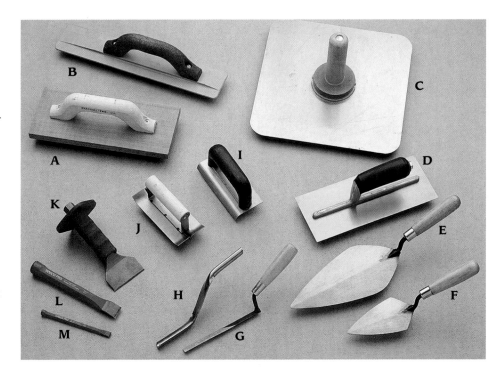

Identifying concrete problems

Problem: Small crack

Small, isolated cracks that extend completely through the slab usually indicate localized problems, such as erosion or settling of the subbase, a weak section in the pour or an insufficient number of control joints. You can fill narrow cracks with liquid crack filler or concrete/mortar repair caulk or liquid (See page 18).

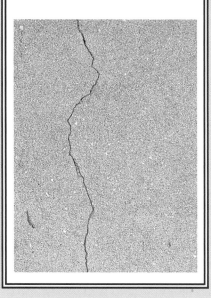

Problem: Multiple cracks

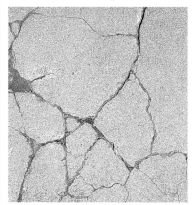

Multiple, larger cracks normally indicate a major subbase problem. One or two large cracks can be repaired to extend the life of a concrete structure, but several larger cracks in a confined area will greatly weaken the structure and repairs will be largely ineffective. To remedy the problem, you'll need to remove the structure, prepare a sturdy subbase with good drainage, and pour new concrete. Fill isolated wide cracks or holes with concrete patching material (See page 19).

Problem: Foundation cracks

Foundation cracks generally indicate settling of one or more foundation walls, which can lead to major structural problems if water penetrates through the crack. Watch them carefully to see if they're getting larger (called *live cracks*). If so, call a foundation repair contractor. Repair cracks in foundation walls with hydraulic cement (See page 31).

Problem: Sunken or heaved concrete

Concrete slabs sink and heave out of position as a result of poor subbase drainage. Excess moisture in the ground causes the soil to expand and contract to a greater degree as the water freezes and thaws. Small-scale problems can sometimes be treated by lifting sunken slabs and backfilling with new concrete (a similar process to mudjacking), but the better solution is to demolish the existing slab, create a new subbase with better drainage, and repour the concrete surface.

Problem: Pop outs

Pop outs occur when aggregate near a concrete surface becomes detached, leaving small voids behind. Causes include under-floating, improper curing and severe freeze/thaw conditions. While pop-outs are common in poured concrete walls and foundations, they occasionally occur in horizontal surfaces as well. Pop-outs are usually of visual concern only and can be filled with commercial vinyl concrete patch if you find them bothersome.

Problem: Potholes (asphalt)

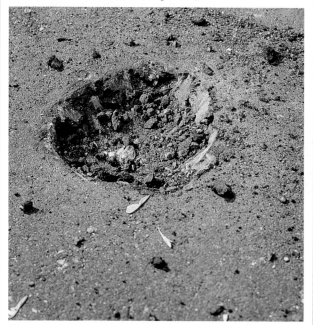

Potholes, like most masonry problems, are caused by changes in temperature and moisture levels, especially when they involve freezing and thawing. Repairing potholes in asphalt is fairly easy—just clean out the hole, add fresh asphalt material and tamp down (See page 25).

Problem: Cracked asphalt

Cracks in asphalt should be of little concern, provided you keep pace with them by repairing them with asphalt sealing compound as soon as they develop (See page 24).

Problem: Failed mortar

Failed mortar joints can be caused by trapped moisture in a brick or block wall, physical stress or a poorly prepared mortar mixture, among other causes. Repair the joints by tuckpointing with fresh mortar before the damage worsens and allows more moisture into the wall (See pages 28 to 29).

Problem: Damaged/missing brick

Bricks and blocks will crack or fracture if exposed to high moisture levels or stress. Very small damaged areas can be patched with mortar patch, but in most cases you'll want to remove and replace the damaged brick (See page 29).

Repairing concrete surfaces

Repairing concrete surfaces (sidewalks, walkways, driveways, garage or basement floors) is mostly a matter of selecting the best repair product for the job, preparing the repair area properly, then applying the products as directed.

Concrete cracks ⅛ in. wide or narrower can simply be filled with concrete and mortar caulk applied with a caulk gun, then smoothed with a putty knife. Concrete caulks are elastomeric (flexible) when dry, so they'll resist minor movement. However, if the crack continues to open up due to faulty construction, caulks should be considered a temporary fix only. Most caulks must be applied to a clean, dry surface and aren't recommended in areas where water pooling occurs, or for subgrade applications (basements and foundations).

A variety of patching products are available for repairing large cracks and holes of various sizes. The products you're most likely to find at your local building center consist of a sand/cement mixture to which you add a bonding liquid or fortifier. Depending on the brand, the bonding agent may be latex, vinyl, acrylic or epoxy. Premixed vinyl-reinforced concrete patching compound is also readily available.

Concrete and concrete repair products are simple to work with because they conform to whatever shape you want them to take on, and they allow plenty of open working time.

How to repair small cracks in concrete surfaces

1 Remove debris from the crack with a putty knife and wire brush, then remove loose material with a shop vac or by spraying with a hose. Wearing rubber gloves, scrub the area around the crack with a solution of 1 cup trisodium phosphate (*TSP*) to 1 gallon of warm water. Rinse thoroughly with clean water and allow to dry.

2 Fill the crack with concrete/mortar repair caulk or liquid, following the label instructions. The caulk should be applied in a continuous bead. Overfill the crack slightly.

3 Seat the bead of caulk into the crack (or smooth off the top surface of poured liquid repair material) by pressing it in with a dampened putty knife. The caulk should be flush to the surrounding surface when tooling is finished.

How to repair large cracks in concrete surfaces

1 Use a hammer and cold chisel to widen and deepen the crack, removing any loose or crumbling concrete. With most patching materials, it helps to undercut the edges slightly to help "key" the patching material into the crack. Some newer products don't require undercutting. Wear heavy gloves and safety goggles to protect yourself from flying chips. Clean the repair area (See *Steps 1 and 2,* previous page).

2 Brush concrete bonding adhesive onto the repair area, including the surfaces surrounding the crack or cracks. The bonding adhesive helps create better adhesion between the repair materials and old concrete surfaces. Allow the bonding adhesive to dry according to the instructions on the label.

3 If the crack or cracks are deeper than ½ in., pack sand into the crack until the surface of the sand is within ½ in. of the concrete surface. Use an old coffee can with a "spout" created by pinching the rim of the can to dispense the sand. Pack the sand into the crack with a thin dowel. The sand simply allows you to conserve more expensive concrete patching compounds. Do not dampen or soak the sand.

4 If using dry-mix material, prepare a stiff mixture of concrete patching material, following the label instructions. Pack the patching compound into the crack with a pointing trowel. Overfill the crack slightly, then strike off the excess so the top of the repair is even with the surrounding concrete surface. Smooth the repair with a trowel. To ensure even curing, keep the patch moist by lightly misting with water several times a day for a week or so. Or, cover the repair area with plastic sheeting.

How to repair holes in concrete surfaces

1 Undercut around the edges of the hole at a slight outward angle. Use a hammer and cold chisel for small holes (See *Step 1, previous page*). For large holes, you can use an angle grinder with a masonry blade (shown above), which is an excellent tool for this task. Or you can use a circular saw equipped with a masonry-cutting blade. In either case, undercut the hole edges. Use a hammer and cold chisel to remove any loose or crumbly material down to sound concrete in the bottom of the hole. On larger holes, like the one above, chip in toward the holes from the undercut edges with the cold chisel. Clean the repair area (See *Step 1, page 18*).

2 Brush on a light coat of concrete bonding adhesive (See *Step 2, previous page*). Add acrylic or latex fortifier to the concrete patching compound (if the compound is not already fortified) and trowel the concrete repair patch material into the hole. For deep holes, pour in and compact a layer of sand to within about 1 in. of the concrete surface (See *Step 3, previous page*), then apply patching compound in several layers, no thicker than ½ in. Allow each layer to set up before applying the next.

3 Use a piece of scrap 2 × 4 as a *screed board* to strike off the top layer of patching material so it's even with the surrounding surface (called *screeding*). Drag the screed board toward yourself in a sawing motion.

4 Use a wood float or a trowel to smooth and feather the surface of the repair (be careful not to overwork the concrete patch). Try to match the surface texture of the surrounding slab. If the surrounding surface has a broomed finish, drag a whisk broom across the wet repair compound in the same direction as the ridges of the surrounding surface. Allow the patch to cure (See *Step 4, previous page*).

How to raise a sunken sidewalk section

Sunken concrete slabs are usually a result of erosion or excess settling of subbase materials. Sections of walks or driveways may heave upward due to pressure from tree roots or ground expansion from frost. On walks, raised or sunken sections may result in trip hazards at expansion joints or off-set cracks across the width of the walk. If the sections are relatively small and the settling isn't too severe, you can often lever them up with a pry bar and either add or remove subbase material to bring the slab back to level. In the case of tree roots, the slab section needs to be removed to create access to the root so it can be cut back out of the way. It's a good idea to check with an arborist before doing this, however. If you're concerned about placing the tree at risk, you can get around the problem by pouring a new slab with a cutout to create space for the adjacent tree.

Large, sunken slabs, such as a driveway, stoop or patio, can often be leveled by a process called "mud jacking" or "slab jacking", which is usually done by a contractor. The procedure involves drilling holes through the low end of the slab, then pumping a cement mixture through the hole into the substrate beneath. As the cement mixture is pumped in, the slab slowly rises back to level. Generally, mud jacking requires specialized skills and equipment, so it's not a do-it-yourself project.

In cases of severe settling or heaving, you may be better off tearing out the entire slab, replacing the subbase and pouring a new slab (or hiring someone to do it).

TIP: Backfilling beneath a sunken concrete slab is a great way to use up leftover concrete from other masonry projects. Before mixing up the concrete, have sunken section propped up and ready to go.

1 Use a wrecking bar and short block to lever up the settled end of the slab (for large slabs, have a helper lever up the opposite side with a second bar). Lift the slab high enough so you can slip a stout wood block underneath it to hold it in position temporarily. Inspect the subbase under the slab—more than likely, the slab has settled into a depression in the subbase (usually sand), due to poor drainage in the subbase. To prevent the raised slab from sinking for the same reason, dig out the subbase area, then refill with a 3- to 4-in.-thick layer of gravel.

2 Prepare a stiff mixture of ordinary concrete to backfill the low area beneath the sunken slab section. Shovel concrete into the low area. Overfill slightly to allow for settling.

3 Raise the concrete section slightly, remove the wood prop, and lower the section back into place. It should be level with, or slightly higher than, the adjoining section. Walk or stomp on the section to set it into the concrete. After a day or two, caulk the expansion or control joints adjoining the section with concrete repair caulk.

How to rebuild a concrete step

Concrete steps often take a bigger beating than other masonry surfaces, due to the constant foot traffic they receive. You can repair cracks, holes and spalling with the same patching materials and techniques as for other concrete surfaces. To repair holes or pop-outs on vertical surfaces, use quick-setting cement or hydraulic cement.

To rebuild a broken or crumbled corner, use latex- or acrylic-fortified concrete patching material or quick-setting cement; some products may require you to prime the area with bonding adhesive; others are two-part mixtures with the bonding agent included. Follow the label directions.

Rebuilt step edges and corners can be reinforced by first driving masonry bolts or screws into the concrete behind the repair area, leaving the head and shank of the fastener protruding into the repair area (but not closer than ½ in. to the surface). You can also drill into the step and drive pieces of rebar into the holes.

1 Cut a ½- to 1-in.-deep groove in the step tread, behind the damaged area, using a circular saw fitted with a masonry blade. The groove should be angled slightly away from the front edge of the damaged step.

2 Clean the repair area (See *Step 1*, page 18). Brush a coat of concrete bonding adhesive onto the damaged step area to provide better adhesion for the repair material.

3 Cut temporary form boards the same width as the step riser height, and prop the form boards in place with heavy bricks or blocks, forming a corner if the damage extends all the way to the end of the step. Pack the void between the forms and the step with concrete repair compound. Add acrylic or latex fortifier to the compound if it is not pre-fortified.

Repairing damaged corners

If a small section of a step corner is damaged, don't try to repair it by re-bonding the missing chunk (as is sometimes suggested). You're better off fixing it by rebuilding the corner in much the same way as the step edge is rebuilt in the sequence shown here.

First, use a hammer and cold chisel to remove any loose or crumbling concrete from the damaged area. Clean the chipped-out area with a wire brush, then clean the surrounding area with *TSP* or concrete cleaner and degreaser. Brush the damaged area with bonding adhesive, if the product you're using calls for it. Mix the concrete patch to a stiff consistency, and apply it to the damaged area with a mason's trowel or wide putty knife, roughly conforming it to shape of the original corner.

While the patch is still wet, cut two pieces of scrap lumber to fit around the corner, then tape them to the step to hold the patch in place. Add more patching material, if needed, and smooth with a trowel. Allow the patch to harden fully before removing boards.

4 Strike off and smooth the patch with a wood concrete float. The float should be riding on the tops of the forms and the step surface as you move it across the repair area in a sawing motion.

5 Allow the patch to harden to the touch, then round over the front edge of the repair with a concrete edging tool or a concrete stair tool (an edging tool is shown above).

6 Use a whisk broom or a float to texture the repair so it matches the texture of the surrounding concrete. Keep the form boards in place until the patch has cured fully (For more information on curing tips, see *Step 4*, page 19).

Repairing cracks in asphalt surfaces

1 Clean out the crack by first scrubbing with a stiff brush and commercial asphalt cleaner, then rinsing with strong spray from a garden hose. Allow the surface to dry thoroughly. Fill deep cracks with sand to within ½ in. of the surface.

Asphalt (also called *blacktop* or *bituminous surface*) is a popular paving material for larger driveways because it is less expensive and more flexible than concrete, which makes it better able to resist minor soil heaving and settling. While asphalt drives require more frequent repair and maintenance, they're much easier to fix. Common repairs include patching cracks and potholes, and sealing the surface every few years to prevent further damage. All are easily accomplished by the do-it-yourselfer. If the asphalt is in good condition but simply needs cleaning, use asphalt driveway cleaner. All patching and sealing compounds perform best when the outside temperature is 60°F or higher. Tools and spills can be cleaned up with mineral spirits.

2 Apply a bead of asphalt sealing compound into the crack, using a caulk gun and overfilling the crack slightly. If the compound is too stiff to squirt in easily (due to cold temperatures) soften it by storing it in a warm room overnight, or by placing it in a sunny location.

3 Use a putty knife or plastic mastic knife to spread and smooth the sealing compound evenly with the surrounding surface. Periodically dip the knife into mineral spirits to keep the compound from sticking. Let the patch cure completely before driving or walking on it.

Sealing asphalt driveways

Liquid asphalt sealer comes in 5-gallon buckets and is applied with a special broom/squeegee or asphalt roller (See photo, right). Asphalt driveways should be resealed every 3 to 4 years—or whenever you notice the surface is starting to develop hairline cracks. Repair all holes and larger cracks before applying the sealer. Also, make sure your car is out of the garage and parked on the street! Wear old clothes, rubber gloves and old shoes you can discard later.

Before applying the sealer, clean the driveway with commercial asphalt driveway cleaner (follow the label directions). Rinse thoroughly and allow the surface to dry. Starting at the garage-end of the driveway, pour out a moderate-sized pool of sealer and spread it evenly over a small section of the driveway. Work the sealer into small cracks. Smooth out the sealer across the asphalt surface, removing any ridges left by the bristles (if using a broom/squeegee).

Continue working in moderate-sized sections until the entire driveway is coated. Allow the sealer to dry for 24 hours (check recommended drying times on the product container label). If, after that time, the sealer is not smooth and uniform, add a second coat. For proper curing and even coverage, two thin coats are better than one thick one. Allow the sealer to cure fully before using the driveway—about two days with most products. Block the drive entrance with sawhorses and rope or "Caution" tape.

Asphalt driveway sealer gives a fresh, new look to older blacktop surfaces. It can be applied with a special roller (above) or a squeegee.

Repairing potholes in asphalt surfaces

1 To fill potholes, remove all loose dirt and debris from the hole. Shallow holes can be cleaned out with a shop vac, then flushed out with a garden hose and spray nozzle. For deeper holes, use a sharp trowel or flat spade to dig down to solid material. Remove any loose asphalt around the hole edges, and cut vertically with a spade or wide cold chisel to clean up the edges of the pothole.

2 Fill the pothole with asphalt (blacktop) patching material. Tamp firmly with a hand tamper. Add additional material as you compress the compound into the hole. Mound the top layer of patch material about ½ in. above the surrounding surface and tamp firmly. To prevent fresh patch material from getting tracked across your driveway or into the house, dust the repair with sand.

Repairing brick & block

While some houses have solid brick or concrete block walls, many modern "brick" homes consist of conventional wood-frame construction with brick siding made of either full-sized bricks or thinner "veneer" bricks. Bricks and concrete blocks are also commonly used for foundations, garden walls and retaining walls. The repair techniques shown here can be used for most brick and block structures. Basic repairs include removing and replacing deteriorated mortar, filling cracks and repairing or replacing damaged bricks and blocks.

The most common problem with older brick and block structures is loose or crumbling mortar joints. These can be repaired by a process known as tuck-pointing. As the term implies, you tuck or pack fresh mortar into the joint with the point of a trowel or a specialized joint-filling tool, then strike the joints smooth. Replacing damaged bricks is another common repair. Surface damage typically occurs when trapped moisture in the brick or block freezes and thaws. If only a few bricks are damaged, you can easily replace them yourself. If you have many bricks to replace in the same area, you should first consult a masonry contractor, especially if you're dealing with a load-bearing wall. Fix small problems before they turn into big ones—if left unchecked, the freezing and thawing of water seeping into small cracks or loose mortar joints will eventually cause more extensive damage to the wall.

A metal bottle opener (sometimes called a church key) is an effective tool for probing mortar joints to inspect the condition of the mortar.

Mixing mortar

The success of any mortar repair project depends greatly on achieving the correct product consistency when mixing. Dampen the mixing container (a mortar tub is shown here), pour in the contents of one bag, add acrylic or latex fortifier in the amount suggested on the fortifier container, then add water until the mixture attains a plastic-like consistency. To test the consistency, slice into the mortar with a trowel—the product should hold its shape and cling to the trowel without crumbling or running off. Some brands of mortar will suggest a general water-to-mortar ratio, but for best results rely on a visual inspection of the first batch you mix, adding incremental amounts of water until the proper consistency is achieved. Keep track of how much water you add to ensure following batches are uniform.

How to repair small cracks in bricks, blocks & mortar joints

1 When occasional hairline cracks or separations develop in brick and block structures, concrete repair caulk may be used to fix the problem. Start by removing any loose material with a small cold chisel. Be careful when working on concrete blocks—even a small cold chisel can cause more damage.

2 Clean out the repair area with a wire brush, then wash with concrete cleaner or a TSP solution (See *Step 1*, page 18). Apply a bead of concrete repair caulk into the crack, overfilling slightly.

3 If repairing a cracked mortar joint, use a mortar grooving tool (V-shaped or U-shaped to match surrounding joints) to force the caulk into the crack and to dress the surface to match the other joints. If repairing a crack in the field area of a brick or block, feather out the caulk with a stiff putty knife.

How to repair a chipped concrete block

1 Clean up the repair area by scrubbing with a wire brush and wiping with TSP or concrete cleaner. Immediately before applying the repair compound, mist the repair area with water (this will prevent the porous concrete block from weakening the patch by drawing out too much moisture).

2 Apply fortified concrete repair compound (add latex or acrylic fortifier to unfortified patching material) with a pointing trowel. Once the patch has set up slightly, strike off the surface with the trowel so it is level with the surrounding block surface. Tool along any mortar lines with a grooving tool to match.

How to tuckpoint failed mortar joints

1 Replacing mortar *(tuckpointing)* is a skill that most do-it-your-selfers can easily master, but it takes a bit of practice. Start your repairs in an inconspicuous area of the brick or block structure until you get the hang of it. First, clean out all loose and crumbling mortar in the repair areas to a depth of ½ to ¾ in. If you're repairing only a few joints, you can use a hammer and cold chisel for all joints; for larger jobs, use a power grinder with a masonry cutoff wheel (an angle grinder is shown above, left) to cut out the mortar from the horizontal joints. Then, use a hammer and a cold chisel to clean out the vertical joints (See photo, above right).

2 Brush any remaining loose mortar from the joints with a stiff bristle brush or wire brush, then vac-uum the joints clean with a shop vac to remove finer particles that can adversely affect the bond of the new mortar. Immediately before applying the new mortar, wet down the repair area.

3 Mix a small batch of mortar (See page 26). Because mortar will dry to a bright gray color, many building restoration specialists add mortar pigment (available from most concrete product suppliers) to the new mortar for a better match with the existing mortar joints. Transfer the wet mortar to a mortar hawk (scrap plywood will work), and use a grooving tool or a pointing trowel to press lines of fresh mortar off the hawk and into the horizontal joints. Wipe up spills immediately.

4 Pack the vertical joints with mortar (don't get ahead of yourself—you'll need to tool the joints before the mortar hardens). Strike off the horizontal joints with a grooving tool (make sure the width and profile match the existing joints). Then strike off and shape the vertical joints with the grooving tool. If your mortar joints are flush with the brick or were treated with a single downward bevel, use a pointing trowel to recreate the effect on the mortar lines, rather than using a grooving tool.

5 Let the mortar dry until the surface is crumbly, then lightly brush off the excess from the tooling process using a nylon-bristled brush. Clean up wet mortar on bricks with a damp burlap rag or abrasive pad. If the mortar has hardened, scrape it off with a stiff plastic putty knife. Keep the new joints damp for several days after the repair by misting lightly with a garden hose once or twice a day.

Variation: How to replace a damaged or missing brick

2 Dampen the replacement brick, apply a layer of mortar to the top and both ends, then slide it into place. TIP: Steady the brick by setting it on a wide piece of scrap wood. Tap the face of the brick with the trowel handle until it is flush with the faces of the other bricks.

3 Scrape off any excess mortar, then tool the joints with a grooving tool to match the existing joints. Keep the mortar damp for several days.

1 Use a hammer and cold chisel to chisel out the old mortar and remaining chunks of the old brick, then clean out the cavity with a strong spray from a garden hose. *NOTE:* As a rule, you should not remove more than four adjoining bricks in one course, especially if you're dealing with a foundation or load-bearing wall. Mix mortar (See page 26) and pack the void with a ⅜ in. thick layer at the back, sides and bottom with a pointing trowel.

Foundation wall repair

The foundation walls of your home must be strong enough to support the weight of the entire structure, in some cases, and to act as a retaining wall to hold back soil around the outside perimeter. Foundation walls, slabs, and basement floors must also be impervious to water—seepage through foundation walls or slabs is a common cause of damp or wet basements and crawl spaces. Sealing foundation walls against water penetration is an important part of the dry-basement equation. You'll also need to provide adequate drainage around the perimeter of your house to direct ground water away from the foundation.

Some masonry waterproofing products can provide effective protection against moisture seepage through the pores of concrete block foundation walls. Repair any visible cracks or damage, then apply the waterproofing product with a brush, stiff broom, roller or spray gun, according to the label instructions. Apply at least two coats.

Tips for reducing condensation

In basements and crawl spaces, condensation is caused by excess humidity and differences in temperature between the air and cool surfaces, such as basement walls and floors or cold water pipes. Below, and on page 32, you will find several tips for controlling condensation.
• In finished basements, remove internal sources of humidity by making sure clothes dryers are vented to the outdoors, repairing leaky faucets and pipes and fixing leaks or seepage problems in walls and floors.
• If, after taking the above measures, the basement is still musty or humid, install a dehumidifier.
• In crawl spaces, cover the ground with a 6-mil poly vapor barrier. Overlap the edges by 6 in., and tape the joints with duct tape. Run the vapor barrier 6 in. up the foundation wall and tape it in place. Weight down the vapor barrier with bricks or pressure-treated 2×4s.

Repairing small cracks in foundation walls

Seal small cracks (less than ⅛ in. wide) with concrete repair caulk (See page 18). Several brands are available in cans and brushed over the cracks or in caulk tubes and are applied with a caulk gun. Follow the label instructions. Be sure to inspect both sides of the wall or walls for cracks. Even hairline cracks may run all the way through the wall. If a crack extends below the ground on the exterior side of the wall, dig down to expose its entire length. Cracks extending completely through poured concrete walls should be sealed on both sides. On hollow-core block walls, seal interior and exterior cracks as you find them. Exterior cracks may cause the hollow cores to fill with water.

Interior

Exterior

Inspecting foundation walls

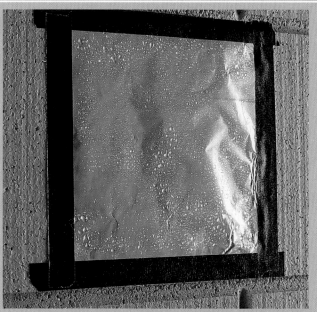

The presence of mildew signals a basement moisture problem.

In addition to regular visual inspections for flaking paint, staining, mildew and other signs of moisture, there are a few simple tests you can perform on your foundation walls. If you have a damp basement, you can determine whether the source is interior or exterior by performing the foil test described to the right. Another useful test is to determine if a crack is "live" (still growing). To test for live cracks, attach one or more microscope slides across the cracks with epoxy glue. If the slides break within a few weeks, this indicates that the crack is growing. If this is the case, seek the advice of a qualified masonry contractor before attempting repairs.

A foil test can be performed on foundation walls to determine the source of a moisture problem. Tape a piece of aluminum foil to the foundation wall (below grade) or basement floor. if the problem is seepage, moisture will form between the foil and the wall; if condensation is the culprit, moisture will form on the outside of the foil. If moisture forms on both sides, the problem may be a combination of the two.

How to repair a large foundation wall crack or hole

1 To repair wide cracks, use hydraulic cement (a product that can be applied effectively to damp or leaking walls). First, prepare the repair area by removing loose debris and cleaning as best you can. Then, mix dry hydraulic cement product with water until it is stiff enough to hold its shape when squeezed (be sure to wear rubber gloves).

2 Shape the hydraulic cement into a ball or rope and press it into the repair area. Add more cement if necessary. Because water actually accelerates the hardening process with hydraulic cement, work quickly—especially if the wall is leaking as you make the repair.

3 Once the hydraulic cement has set up, scrape off any excess with a wet trowel. Feather the edges of the patch into the wall surface as best you can. *NOTE:* Hydraulic cement is generally used as an emergency measure for active leaks. If the hole in the wall is above grade or leaking, you can use standard concrete repair products.

Quick tips for damp basements

Insulate cold water pipes using adhesive-backed insulating tape for short runs, or slit foam sleeves (above photo) for longer runs. While you're at it, also insulate hot water pipes to save on energy costs.

Install foundation vents in homes with a crawlspace or unheated basement. Provide at least 1 square ft. of open vent space for every 150 ft. of floor space (allow for reduced airflow due to vent screens or insect screening). Space vents no more than 25 ft. apart. Place vents across from one another on opposite walls to ensure good cross-ventilation.

How to insulate a foundation wall

1 After correcting any seepage or leakage problems attach 1 × 2 furring strips to the foundation wall, 24 in. on-center (attach the strips to nailers at the sole and cap of the wall, and apply construction adhesive to the backs of the furring strips). Cut and fit rigid foam insulation panels between the strips, and attach the insulation with construction adhesive or the adhesive type recommended by the insulation board manufacturer.

2 Staple a 6-mil poly vapor barrier to the furring strips to cover the entire wall surface. Finish the installation with wallboard, paneling or another similar wallcovering of your choice. *NOTE:* Most building codes require that rigid foam insulation in living spaces be covered as a fire-retarding measure.

Anatomy of a subsurface drainage system

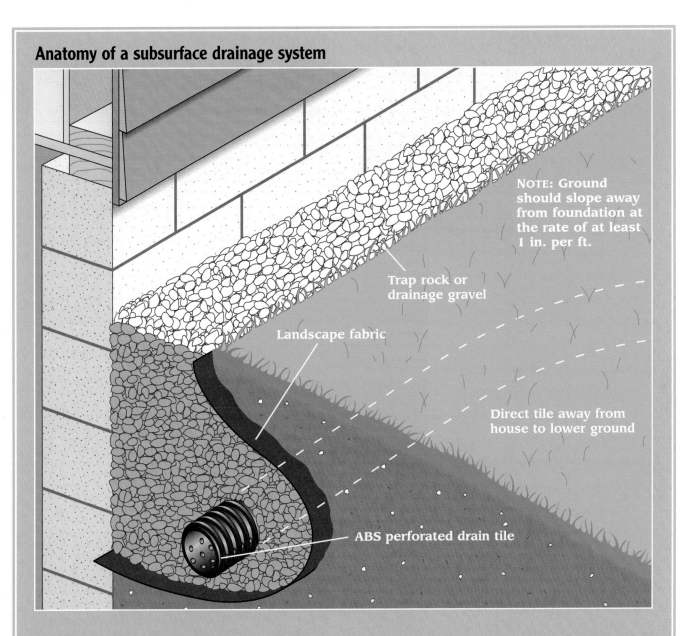

NOTE: Ground should slope away from foundation at the rate of at least 1 in. per ft.

Trap rock or drainage gravel

Landscape fabric

Direct tile away from house to lower ground

ABS perforated drain tile

Subsurface drainage systems consist of interconnecting clay drain tiles or perforated ABS drain pipes placed in a gravel trench around the outside perimeter of foundation footings. The pipes collect ground water at the base of the foundation and route it to a dry well, sewer, storm drain, gutter or other outfall location. These systems are usually installed when the house is built. But, if your foundation doesn't have one, and other waterproofing methods have failed, you should install one.

If the foundation footing is only a few feet underground, you can do the work yourself, but still be prepared for a lot of shovel work. If the house has a basement, you're better off hiring an excavation contractor to do the digging, or hire out the entire job.

To make a subsurface drainage system, start by digging a trench next to the foundation wall, at least a couple of feet deep. Ideally, the trench should extend as deep as the foundation footing. Run landscape fab-

ric along the bottom and up the side of the trench (this will keep the surrounding earth from leaching into and possibly plugging the drain tile holes). Add a 1- to 2-in.-deep layer of coarse drainage gravel or trap rock to the bottom of the trench. Lay clay drain tiles or ABS perforated drain tile on the gravel base,about 1 ft. away from and parallel to the foundation wall. At the low end, extend the pipe away from the house and trench it toward the outfall location.

Backfill the trench with gravel to within 1 ft. of grade. If you do not want to have exposed gravel visible next to the house, extend the fabric over the top of the gravel and cover with topsoil. Otherwise fill the trench to the top with gravel. Make sure the end of the drain tile is clear and drains to a suitable outfall area.

Repairing Siding

Siding is designed to shed water, protect the wall framing members and interior wall surfaces and to improve the appearance of your home. Cracks, holes, splits, open joints and other forms of damage to siding allow water to enter, accelerating the declining condition of the siding and creating the potential for major structural problems inside the walls. The key to maintaining a weather-tight wall and extending siding life is to spot and correct small problems before they turn into big ones.

This chapter covers simple repairs to common types of siding. If the damage is so extensive or widespread that the house needs residing, consider hiring a contractor to do the work. However, a bit of preventative maintenance goes a long way toward extending the life of the wall. In addition to regular inspections of the siding (See pages 156 to 157), wash the exterior of your house at least once a year to keep the surface free of dirt, mold and mildew. A rented pressure washer makes the chore much less tedious. Other frequent maintenance repairs include touching up paint, repairing minor holes and dents, reattaching loose boards or panels and resetting popped-out nails.

Tips for maintaining siding

✔ Caulk all joints and seams between siding and trim, and between board ends with exterior-grade, paintable acrylic latex or siliconized acrylic caulk. These caulks come in a variety of colors that make repairs less conspicuous. Otherwise, touch up caulk lines with matching paint.

✔ Fill small nail holes, dents, cracks and joints (less than 1/16 in. wide) with exterior wood filler. To fill a dent, rough up the area with sandpaper and apply filler with a wide putty knife. Sand smooth with sandpaper and a sanding block. Paint or stain immediately.

✔ Patch larger holes or rotted areas with exterior wood filler or two-part epoxy wood filler. For details on applying the filler, see pages 58 to 59.

✔ To reattach a loose board, carefully pry up the board at nail locations with a flat pry bar. With a caulk gun, apply liberal dabs of construction adhesive at nail locations behind the board. Then, reset the original nails. If the nails won't hold, drive an additional nail or galvanized deck screw about 1 in. above the original ones (use rust-resistant spiral or ring-shank siding nails).

Common siding problems

Problem: Rotten siding

Wood rot is common on siding and trim, especially at corners and near roof lines. Minor rot can be repaired (pages 58 to 59). Larger rotten areas require replacement (pages 36 to 37).

Problem: Delamination & swelling

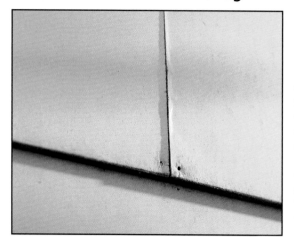

Delamination and swelling occur when moisture penetrates manufactured wood-based siding products, such as hardboard. The siding swells, which causes nails to pop out or sink and disintegrates or delaminates the siding materials. Warping can also occur from the swelling pressure. Replace damaged boards (pages 36 to 37).

Problem: Dented metal siding

Dents and dings in metal siding may be repairable with resin-based wood filler products, but the best solution is to patch or replace the siding strips (page 47). Because dents are not likely to lead to larger problems, you may choose to accept and live with the problem.

Problem: Hole in vinyl

Small holes and tears in vinyl siding can occur for a variety of reasons. Patch (page 46) or replace (pages 44 to 45) the affected siding strip.

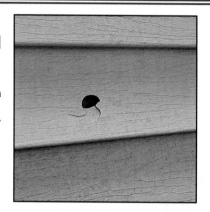

Problem: Cracked stucco

Narrow cracks in stucco siding should be repaired as soon as they're detected, since they can spread quickly. Concrete or stucco repair caulk is normally used for this type of repair (page 48). Holes and wide cracks should be patched with concrete repair compound (page 49). Persistent problems indicate that a moisture problem exists. Inspect flashings and interior walls for additional signs that help identify the source of the problem.

Problem: Missing shakes

Wood shakes and shingles are relatively high-maintenance siding materials since they have so many exposed edges. Rot or even high winds can cause the shakes, or even whole sections of shakes, to fall off. Replace the materials (pages 40 to 41 and 96).

Reset popped nails with a hammer and nailset. Countersink nail heads and fill the holes with exterior wood filler. Be careful not to split the wood at board ends—if possible, remove the nails and replace them with longer ones.

Wood siding

Although wood remains one of the most popular siding materials, it also requires more frequent maintenance and repair than other siding types. Dry rot, splitting and warping, peeling or blistering paint and damage from pests, including termites, are some of the problems you may eventually have to deal with. However, most repairs are relatively easy to make, requiring only basic skills and a few everyday tools. As with other types of siding, water or moisture penetration is the greatest enemy to wood siding and the wall behind. Identify and correct the source of the moisture damage before making repairs. Common wood siding types include: beveled lap siding (usually cedar, pine or hardboard), vertical sheet siding, tongue-and-groove horizontal strip siding, and wood shakes (shingles).

Matching materials

Wood siding types don't change as often as metal or vinyl lap siding, but it's possible that you won't be able to find an exact match for your existing siding at your local building center. In this case, choose the style that matches most closely and rip it to width if necessary. If the repair area is in a high-visibility area of your house, "borrow" siding from a less visible spot and use it to make the repair. Replace the "borrowed" siding with the new material.

How to replace damaged lap siding

Minor damage to wood lap siding can be repaired using exterior wood filler (See pages 58-59) or a wood patch. But wood lap siding with more extensive damage should be replaced, especially when the damage involves multiple pieces of siding. Because lap siding has distinctive lines created by the laps, the most satisfactory repairs are brought about by replacing larger sections of siding (this minimizes the number of vertical seams that distract from the horizontal lines). Where possible, try to remove and replace complete boards. But if you must cut out a section to replace, be sure to make your cuts at wall framing member locations so both sides of the vertical seam can be nailed securely.

1 Mark vertical cutting lines on each side of the damaged area using a combination square and pencil. To blend in with the siding pattern, avoid removing sections that are less than 4 ft. long. The cutting line should fall over wall framing member locations (use the existing nailing patterns or an electronic stud finder as a reference to find the locations). If you're replacing more than one board, stagger the cutting lines.

2 Carefully pull out any nails along the bottom of the damaged board, then drive wood shims beneath the board to prop it away from the board below. Press a scrap board against the bottom edge of the board to be cut so the saw doesn't damage the siding below the work area. Use a backsaw to cut through the board along the cutting lines. Stop the cut near the top of the board to prevent gouging the board above.

3 Remove the shims, then tap them beneath the siding board above the damaged section to expose the top of the damaged board. Finish the cuts with a keyhole saw or wallboard saw, and remove the damaged section (if the board won't come out easily, split it into several pieces with a chisel). Work carefully to avoid damaging building paper or sheathing behind the siding. Pry out any nails that will block the replacement board (or trim them off with a hacksaw blade slipped beneath the siding).

TIP: In most wall situations, the sheathing behind the siding is covered with building paper that functions primarily as a vapor barrier. If the building paper layer behind the repair area is damaged or brittle, repair or replace it. You can patch small tears or nail holes in felt with fiber-reinforced roof cement. For larger holes or damaged sections, remove the old paper, then cut a replacement patch slightly larger than the damaged area. Slip the top edge of the patch under the seam above the repair area, and nail or staple in place. Apply roof cement at the ends of the repair.

4 Cut new siding to fit the opening, allowing for a ⅛-in. expansion gap at each end. Coat the new board with exterior primer or clear wood preservative. Slip the replacement piece underneath the siding above and nail in place with ring-shank siding nails, copying the existing nailing pattern if possible. If replacing more than one board, begin by installing the lowest board and work toward the top. Set the nailheads and fill the holes with exterior wood filler. Apply caulk in the joints where boards butt together.

1

How to repair cracked lap siding

Wood lap siding offers many advantages over other siding materials (most of them are aesthetic), but it also presents one or two unique possibilities for damage. Because the boards are sawn from natural lumber, they contain distinctive grain lines that can lead to splitting or cracking under stress. If a siding board is cracked or split along its entire length, it's best to replace the whole board. If the board is split only part way, it can be repaired with exterior glue.

1 On horizontal siding, remove the nails below the split area (if any); on vertical siding, remove the nails (and batten, if any) on the side closest to the split.

2 Pry the crack open slightly with a chisel, if necessary, to create access for the glue bottle tip. Apply polyurethane glue (the best choice) or ordinary water-resistant wood glue into the crack, making sure the wood on both sides of the crack is coated.

2

3 On horizontal siding, cut a 1×4 slightly longer than the length of the crack; position it under the bottom lap of the damaged board and force the 1×4 upward to press the crack closed. If working close to the ground, wedge 2×4s under the 1×4 to hold it in place; otherwise, temporarily tack the board to the wall with deck screws. Clean off any glue squeeze-out before it sets. Once the glue has cured, remove the 1×4 brace and touch up, as needed, along the crack with matching exterior paint or stain.

VARIATION: For vertical siding, force the crack closed with a flat pry bar or chisel, then wedge wood shims into the joint between the damaged board and the adjacent piece of siding. Clean off any glue squeeze-out. When the glue dries, drive 8d galvanized finish nails on each side of the crack at nailing locations. Set the nailheads, fill the nail holes with exterior wood filler and touch up the repair with matching exterior paint.

3

How to repair tongue-and-groove siding

Tongue-and-groove siding is less susceptible to rot than wood lap siding because the seams are tighter and there is less edge-grain exposure. But like any type of wood siding, it's vulnerable to damage from pests or accidental blows. Small areas of damage or rot can be repaired with wood filler (See pages 58 to 59). For extensive damage, remove the damaged board or boards and replace them. This process is similar to the repair methods for other types of wood siding but is complicated a little by the tongues and grooves.

1 To remove a damaged section of tongue-and-groove siding, mark cutting lines centered over the nearest wall framing members on each side of the damaged area. Remove any interfering nails. Set your circular saw blade to cut about 1 in. deeper than the siding thickness, and make "pocket-style" plunge cuts (starting and stopping inside the edges of the adjoining boards) along the cutting lines. If removing more than one board, stagger the cuts.

2 Complete the cuts at each end with a mallet and sharp wood chisel. Split the cut-out section lengthwise with the chisel, and carefully pry out from the center with a flat pry bar to remove the siding pieces. Also remove any nails from the repair area.

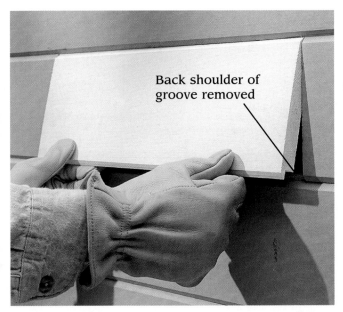

Back shoulder of groove removed

3 Cut a new piece (or pieces) of siding to length, then pare off the back shoulder of the grooved edge of each patch board, using a chisel. Prime the board and slip it into the repair opening so the "tongue" edge fits into the groove in the board above it and the front shoulder of the grooved edge covers the tongue on the board below (if replacing multiple boards, start at the bottom).

4 Attach the patches by driving 8d galvanized common nails (or ring-shank siding nails) at stud locations. Set the nailheads below the surface and fill the holes with exterior wood filler. Apply caulk at the seams at each end, and paint the patch board or boards to match the surrounding siding.

Replacing damaged wood shakes & shingles

Wood shakes and shingles are common siding products for entire houses—for example, on shingle-covered Victorian houses (called *Stick-style*). They're also installed on second stories of lap-sided homes built around the 1920s, as well as on additions to homes of many styles. Repairing damaged or missing siding shingles is mostly a matter of finding replacement materials and installing them to match the original installation technique.

Cedar shingles and shakes are graded according to standard quality measures. *Grade 1* and *Grade 2* materials are free of knots, cracks and other damage. They're used for exposed surfaces on both walls and roofs. *Grade 3* and *Grade 4* are lesser grades normally used for starter courses and other areas that are covered by better quality materials. Surface textures also vary in degrees of roughness. Bring along a sample when buying replacements.

1 Remove damaged shingles by splitting them into several narrow strips with a hammer and chisel, then pulling or prying the strips from the wall surface.

Shims

2 Slip a hacksaw blade under the undamaged shingle above the repair area and cut off any protruding nailheads. If necessary, shim out the top shingle slightly to provide clearance for the saw.

3 Measure and cut a shingle to fit the space, allowing a ¼-in. expansion gap along each side. If you need to cut the shingle to width, mark a cutting line and score it several times with a utility knife, then bend the shingle to snap it. Slip the thin end of the new shingle under the shingle above the repair area, until the lower "butt" edge is ¼ to ⅜ in. below the adjoining shingles in the course. Drive two 5d galvanized nails (common or siding) through the new shingle at a downward angle, as close as possible to the shingle course above the repair area (use 8d nails for shakes or thicker shingles). Drive the nailheads flush with the surface, then cover with a dab of clear silicone caulk.

4 Slip a wood block beneath the butt end of the shingle and rap upward on the block with a hammer. The force will drive the shingle and nails upward. Hammer until the bottom of the shingle is flush with surrounding shingles and the nailheads are hidden behind the shingle course above.

Repairing corner shakes & shingles

Most houses with wood shingle or shake siding feature corners formed with the same materials used for the field shingles (rather than trim boards like those used with other types of wood siding). While they preserve the appearance of the rest of the walls, corner shingles are more susceptible to physical damage than the field shingles. Replacing damaged corner shingles is quite similar to replacing field shingles. The primary difference is that the corners are created by lapping one corner shingle over the exposed edge of the mating corner shingle. The lapping shingle alternates from side to side on successive courses to minimize side-grain exposure and create a more appealing layout.

Shakes or shingles?

The terms "shakes" and "shingles" are often used interchangeably because the products are quite similar and the techniques used to install and repair them are identical. The difference (which you should be aware of when purchasing replacement materials) is that shingles are sawn to size so they have more uniform dimensions and are generally smaller and smoother on the surfaces and edges. Shakes are split to rough size, making them less regular in appearance. Both can be purchased at most building centers and lumberyards.

1 Remove the damaged shingles and nails as you would remove field shingles (See previous page). Starting at the bottom of the repair area, cut one new corner shingle to fit, allowing an expansion gap of ¼ in. on the field side and overhanging the corner by the thickness of one shingle. Nail this shingle in place with 5d or 8d galvanized nails.

2 Cut and fit the mating shingles for the opposite side of the corner so it will butt tightly against the first new shingle installed. Apply a thin bead of silicone caulk to the mating edge of the shingle, then nail it to the wall so the mating edge butts tightly against the first shingle to form the corner. Clean up any excess caulk.

3 Install the rest of the replacement shingles. The side of the overhanging shingle should alternate every other course. Install the singles at the highest course of the replacement area using the same technique shown in Steps 3 and 4 on the previous page.

Fixing board-and-batten siding

Board-and-batten siding is composed of vertical strips or panels, usually of rough-sawn exterior wood siding. The seams between strips or panels are covered with wood battens (often made from 1×2 or 1×3 lumber) for a rustic appearance. Repairs usually are made by removing and replacing damaged siding or battens. Small damaged areas can be fixed with wood filler (See pages 58 to 59).

1 Using a pry bar, carefully remove any battens covering the damaged board or boards. Pry off the damaged siding, removing nails as you go. If the nails pull out with the board, catch the nail shank behind the board with the flat end of your pry bar, and tap the board down with a hammer or the palm of your hand to expose the head, then remove the nails.

2 To replace a section of the damaged board, trim off the deteriorated area with a circular saw set to cut at a 30° bevel. If the siding was attached to horizontal nailing strips, make the cut so it falls over one of the strips. Reattach the section of siding you're saving with the beveled end at the joint created in the repair area. Use 8d galvanized siding or ring-shank nails to attach the board.

Patch board

3 Cut the replacement board section from matching stock. The end of the patch piece should be cut with a 30° bevel from the opposite direction to form a scarf joint with the original piece of siding. Prime and paint the patch to match the siding. Apply a bead of construction adhesive or exterior caulk to the beveled end of the old siding board, then slip the patch into position so the beveled ends fit together tightly.

4 Apply exterior caulk in the joints between the patch board and the existing siding, then reattach the battens so they're centered over the vertical joints (do not use the old nail holes). Set the nailheads and cover with exterior wood filler. Touch-up the paint on the battens as needed.

Repairing asbestos siding

If your home was built or remodeled between 1930 and 1970, it may contain asbestos siding. Asbestos shingles resemble wood shingles in appearance, but have a glossier "fiberglass" type surface and are generally uniform in size and shape. Because asbestos was determined to be a dangerous carcinogen, the manufacture of these products was outlawed and handling them is now subject to strict regulations (See *Warning* below). It is unlikely that you'll be able to find replacement shingles that are an exact match for repairing asbestos siding, but you can probably find modern cement- or fiberglass-based shingles that are close in size and style.

WARNING

Building products containing asbestos are potential health hazards subject to regulations governing proper removal and disposal. In many areas, homeowners are allowed to handle these products in limited amounts, provided the proper safety precautions are followed. Typically, larger projects must be handled by licensed asbestos abatement contractors. Always check with your local building department before beginning any project involving asbestos materials, and follow their recommendations for handling and disposal.

1 As a safety precaution, thoroughly dampen the damaged shingle or shingles with a mixture of 1 ounce dishwashing soap to 8 ounces of water, applied with a spray bottle. Repeat throughout the repair procedure, making sure the shingles do not dry out. When handling or applying tools to the asbestos shingles, protect yourself by wearing heavy gloves, long-sleeved shirt and pants and a MSHA-NIOSH approved respirator for asbestos (available at hardware stores).

2 Break apart the damaged shingle with a hammer and cold chisel and pull or cut the nails. If nailheads are covered by the shingle course above, slip a hacksaw blade under the shingles above the repair area and cut the nails. Be careful not to damage surrounding shingles. Place all pieces of the shingles in a sealable plastic storage bag for temporary storage before disposing according to local environmental regulations.

3 Slip the new shingle under the siding course above and hold in place. Use a drill fitted with a carbide bit to drill new nail pilot holes near the old nail holes. Drive 4d galvanized ring shank or spiral nails flush to the surface (do not countersink). Touch up nailheads with clear silicone caulk or matching paint.

Common problems associated with vinyl siding include cracks, holes, color fading and damage to corner caps or strips. As a rule, vinyl siding cannot be repainted, but check with the siding manufacturer. Usually, it's best to replace the entire damaged panel. Or, you can cut out and replace just the damaged section if the resulting seams aren't objectionable. Generally, don't try to repair damaged areas with caulks or other patching materials, as the repair often looks worse than the original damage.

Metal siding won't crack, but is subject to dents. Small dents are best left alone, especially on "fake wood grain" types.

Buckling or warping of both types is usually a result of improper installation. In most cases, the panels were either nailed too tightly to the sheathing or not enough clearance was left between panel ends or corners. In the case of vinyl siding, you may be able to correct the problem by removing the affected panels, trimming the ends to provide clearance and renailing them to the wall. Metal panels are difficult to remove and reuse without causing permanent denting or kinking. If you have major buckling problems, consult a siding contractor (but first check your warranty).

Styles and colors change regularly with manufactured siding, often making it difficult to obtain matching replacement pieces. Generally, the best source is through specialty siding distributors. If distributors do not have the right material in stock, they may be willing to order it for you. If all else fails, find the closest match you can and use original material from a low-visibility area of the house to replace the damaged siding. Then, replace the removed siding with the near-match material.

Metal/vinyl siding cross-section

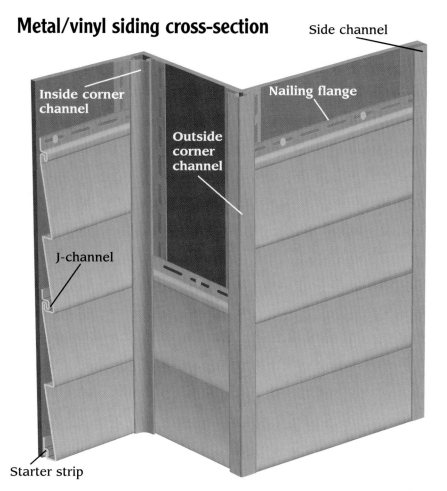

Inside corner channel

Outside corner channel

J-channel

Starter strip

Side channel

Nailing flange

Vinyl, aluminum and steel siding products are installed using similar fittings, fasteners and techniques. Most often, they're attached directly over the exterior wall sheathing. The ends and corners are fitted into trim fittings that contain channels.

How to replace a vinyl siding strip

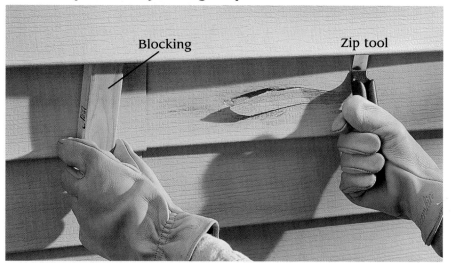

Blocking

Zip tool

1 To remove a damaged panel, first unlock the bottom edge of the strip or strips above the damaged panel, using a *zip tool* (a specialty tool available at siding dealers and some building centers). Starting at one end, hook the tool under the lip and slide it along the length of the strip while pulling downward and outward slightly. Insert blocking into the open joint to prevent the lap joint from reconnecting.

2 With a flat pry bar, remove the nails from the nailing flange at the top of the damaged piece. A wood block will increase prying leverage and prevent damage to adjoining siding strips. Remove the damaged siding.

3 Cut a piece of replacement siding to the same length as the damaged piece (use a power miter saw or a sharp utility knife with a straightedge cutting guide to cut vinyl siding). Snap the bottom lip of the replacement piece over the mating lip of the top of the siding strips beneath the repair area.

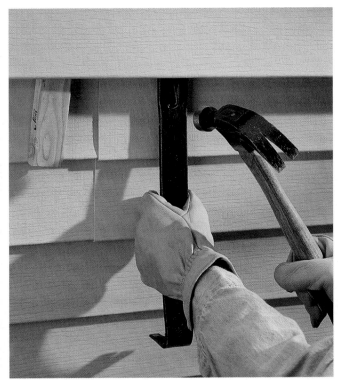

4 Attach the top edge by driving 3d galvanized ring shank or siding nails through the centers of the slots on the nailing flange and into the sheathing. Do not drive the nails too tightly. If you have trouble accessing the nails, position the end of a pry bar over the nailhead and drive it in by tapping the end of the pry bar with a hammer.

5 Lock the lower lip of the siding strips in the course above to the new strip, using the zip tool.

How to replace a small section of vinyl siding

1 Unlock the panel above the damaged area with a zip tool and remove the nails from the flange of the damaged section (See *Steps 1 and 2,* pages 44 and 45). With a sharp utility knife and a straightedge, cut out the damaged section (several passes may be required). Start by cutting through the panel down to the top edge of the J-channel on the damaged piece. Then unlock the channel with your zip tool, wedge it out, and finish the cut.

2 Cut a replacement piece that's 4 in. longer than the cut-out section, then trim 2¼ in. of the nailing flange off each end of the piece. Slip the replacement piece into position, then nail it in place (See *Steps 3 and 4,* page 45). Relock the strip above, using your zip tool, if necessary.

How to repair a vinyl siding strip

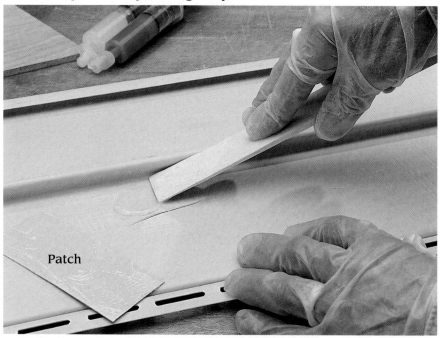

Patch

1 Remove the damaged panel and place it face-down on a flat surface. If the face of the siding is discolored or rough, cut out around the damage with scissors or snips. From the same (or similar) materials the siding, cut a patch slightly wider and longer than the damaged area. Thoroughly clean the siding around the damaged area, then apply two-part epoxy glue around the repair area. Also apply glue to the front (textured) face of the patch. Take care not to coat patch surfaces that will be visible.

2 Immediately after coating the surfaces, press the patch in place, good side down. After the glue dries, reinstall the panel (See *Steps 3 to 5,* page 45).

Patching aluminum or steel siding

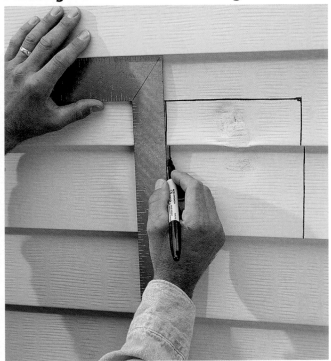

1 Mark a rectangular or square cutout around the damaged portion of the panel. Leave at least 2 in. of surface area between the top of the cut-out area and the siding lap above it to serve as a bonding surface for the siding patch. Cut out the damaged area with aviator snips and a hacksaw blade. Light-gauge aluminum siding can be cut with a sharp utility knife.

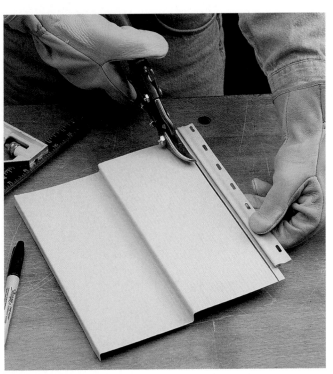

2 Cut a patch from matching siding, 3 in. wider than the cut-out area. The patch should be long enough that the top edge fits under the course above it when the patch is installed. Cut off the nailing flange with aviator snips or a straightedge and sharp utility knife. Smooth-out (deburr) rough edges on the cutting line with 180-grit silicon carbide sandpaper.

3 Rough up (scarify) the back of the patch with the sandpaper, then wipe it clean. Also clean the mating area on the siding. Apply clear silicone caulk to the back of the patch, making sure the perimeter is well covered.

4 Lock the J-channel on the bottom edge of the patch over the adjacent J-channel on the existing siding, while slipping the top edge under the course above. Press in place. Wipe off any squeezed-out caulk at seams with a rag and mineral spirits.

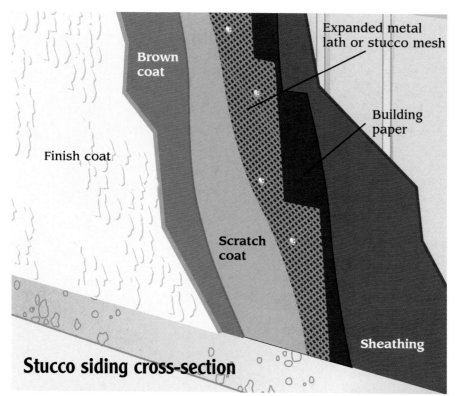

Brown coat

Expanded metal lath or stucco mesh

Building paper

Finish coat

Scratch coat

Sheathing

Stucco siding cross-section

Stucco is a cementitious siding product applied over wood-framed or masonry walls. It is generally applied in three layers (the *scratch coat*, the *brown coat* and the *finish coat*), with the first layer embedded in expanded metal lath or stucco mesh to hold the siding to the wall. Making repairs to stucco is similar to making basic concrete repairs (See pages 14 to 23).

Stucco siding

Stucco is the original low-maintenance siding material. But still, problems can occur in stucco, including cracking (especially around window and door frames) and chipped or missing stucco (usually at wall corners, due to physical damage). Small cracks (up to ¼ in. wide) can be filled with concrete or stucco repair caulk or siliconized acrylic caulk that closely matches the stucco color. Patch wider cracks and small holes with a stucco patching compound or concrete repair compound. Repairing major damage, including large holes and widespread cracks, is a job best left to an experienced stucco contractor—in most cases, the damage occurs due to moisture penetration. The source of the moisture must be located and eliminated for the repair to last.

How to patch narrow cracks in stucco

1 Fill cracks up to ¼ in. wide with siliconized acrylic caulk in a matching color or textured concrete repair caulk. A few building centers and masonry products dealers stock special stucco repair caulk, which is similar to concrete repair caulk in composition, but usually blends in better with the stucco surface. Clean out the crack with a stiff wire brush, then apply the caulk with a caulk gun, overfilling the crack slightly.

2 Force the caulk into the crack with a putty knife (coating the knife blade with mineral spirits will prevent the caulk from sticking and pulling out). Smooth the repair so it's flush with the surrounding surface. Wipe up any excess caulk on either side of the crack with a damp sponge or rag. If your stucco has been painted, touch up the repair with matching paint.

How to patch a hole in stucco

1 Use a hammer and cold chisel to knock loose and remove any deteriorated stucco around the damaged area. Also use the chisel to undercut the edges of the hole at a slight inward angle (this will prevent the patch from falling out after it dries). Use a gentle touch to avoid causing any further damage to the stucco or the underlaying sheathing and metal lath.

2 Clean the repair area and surrounding stucco with a wire brush. Be careful not to damage the metal lath or building paper behind. NOTE: If the stucco is applied over a masonry wall, clean off any loose material with a wire brush and coat the surface with latex bonding liquid (See *page 19*).

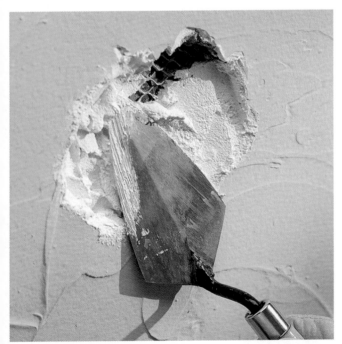

3 Fill the hole with stucco patch (available powdered or premixed at most building centers). If the hole is more than ½ in. deep or extends all the way to the lath, build up the patch in several layers (check the product label instructions—application techniques vary).

4 As the final layer of stucco patch sets up, smooth the surface with a masonry trowel or float, feathering it onto the surrounding wall. Use a whisk broom or bristle brush for walls with a stippled texture. A metal trowel or float, or even a wallboard knife, can be used to create the whorled texture shown above. Let the patch cure according to the label instructions, then paint to match the surrounding wall on painted walls with a paint formulated for use over stucco.

Repairing Windows & Doors

Because exterior doors and most windows are the "movable" parts of a house exterior, they take the worst beating. They're subject to physical abuse from constant opening and closing, as well as weather-related damage from condensation, wind-driven rain and snow, exposure to direct sunlight and temperature changes. Also, settling of the house can result in out-of-square frames, causing windows or doors to operate poorly.

Due to these constant assaults, window and door replacement is one of the more common home remodeling projects. Even so, you can extend the life of these important (and often expensive) home features by inspecting and maintaining them regularly and making minor repairs as needed. When examining a window or door, make sure the paint and weatherstripping are in good shape, gaps around the exterior trim are well sealed with caulk, and that hardware, screening and window glass are in good repair. Also be on the lookout for wood rot and pest infestation, including termite problems (See page 147). Fix any problems you discover before the damage becomes more severe.

Most basic window and door repairs described in this chapter can be accomplished in an afternoon or less. For details on caulking and weatherstripping doors and windows, see pages 132 to 142.

Materials for repairing windows & doors

Materials and products used frequently in window and door repair include:
(A) exterior wood filler (polyester resin based—for more long-lasting repairs use two-part epoxy filler); **(B)** glazing compound (tube cartridge for easy dispensing); **(C)** glazing compound (quart container product is rolled into glazing "ropes" before application); **(D)** siliconized acrylic caulk; **(E)** 100% silicone caulk; **(F)** wood glue (moisture-resistant); **(G)** turn buttons for securing storm/screen windows; **(H)** window hanger clips for installing and storing storm/screen windows; **(I)** snap clips for securing storm/screen windows; **(J)** glazier's points; **(K)** roll-type window glazing.

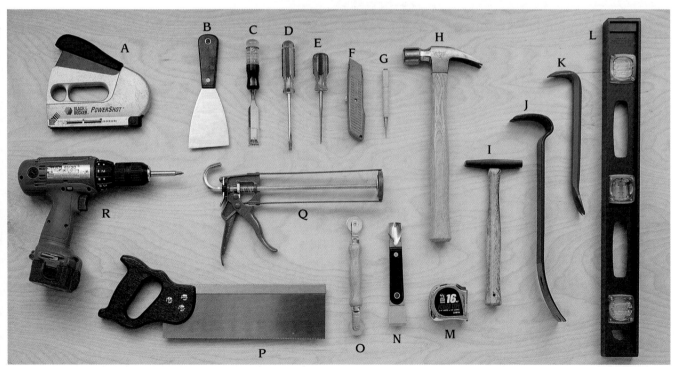

Tools for repairing windows & doors

The above assortment of hand tools and specialty tools can be used to complete just about any window or door repair you need to make:
(A) staple gun; **(B)** stiff putty knife (1½-in. blade); **(C)** wood chisel; **(D)** slotted screwdriver; **(E)** scratch awl; **(F)** utility knife; **(G)** nailset; **(H)** claw hammer; **(I)** tack hammer; **(J)** flat pry bar; **(K)** "cat's paw" pry bar; **(L)** two-foot carpenter's level; **(M)** tape measure; **(N)** window glazing knife; **(O)** spline roller (for use with metal sash frames); **(P)** back saw; **(Q)** caulk gun; **(R)** drill/driver.

Identifying window & door problems

Problem: Failed glazing

Failed glazing is more than simply an eyesore around your window panes. In addition to helping hold the glass in place, glazing also creates a seal that inhibits air transfer between your home and the outdoors. Reglazing a window is a basic skill that anyone who owns a home with wood-frame windows will eventually need to do (See page 64).

Problem: Damaged screening

Screen damage can be caused by many forces, from accidental kicks to tossed newspapers to ordinary deterioration from time and exposure to the elements. Repair these unsightly blemishes on your home by replacing the window screening (See pages 67 to 69).

Problem: Cracked glass

Cracked glass weakens windows and allows outside air into your home. Whether your windows have wood or metal sash frames, replacing a glass pane is relatively simple. In many cases, it can be accomplished without removing the window sash from the window (See pages 63 to 65).

Problem: Worn threshold

Door thresholds are subject to constant wear and will eventually need replacement. Even newer metal thresholds are subject to sags, dents and other types of wear. In addition to allowing pest and outside air air entry, a worn threshold may cause premature deterioration of the wood sill below. Replace thresholds and sills as soon as damage becomes evident (See pages 71 to 72).

Problem: Broken metal sash

Metal sash frames can be found in most operating windows installed in recent years. While they're lighter and not subject to rot, they can rust or the corner joints can fail. Because

they are so inexpensive, it is tempting to simply replace the metal sash with a new unit. But if you are a little more resourceful and ambitious, you can repair metal sash frames easily, as long as you can locate corner hardware fittings that match (See page 65).

Problem: Failed wood sash:

Wood sash frames can fail for a variety of reasons, including rot caused by moisture exposure, a poor protective finish or racking caused by settling of the house that throws the window frame out of square. In most cases, frames can be repaired or rebuilt once they're removed from the window (See page 57).

Problem: Deteriorated brickmold

Brickmold trim around the exterior of windows and doors is not simply decorative. Like many types of house trim, it protects the interior of the wall and the door or window framing from moisture. Blistered paint and visible rot are signals that your brickmold should be replaced (See page 73).

Problem: Damaged jambs & casework

Jambs and casework are frequent victims to rot, stress and even even pest infestation, like the termite-infested door casing shown above. While repairing or replacing this type of trim, it's important that you identify and eliminate the source of the damage (See page 70).

Problem: Deteriorated window sill

Window sills are among the most likely spots to find wood rot and other forms of damage on the exterior of your home. Not only does their flat surface make them more susceptible to pro-

longed moisture exposure, their proximity to the condensation often caused by the mingling of warm and cold air creates an additional moisture source that can lead to rot. If detected in its early stages, rot can be repaired with exterior wood filler (See pages 58 to 59). But sills with more extensive damage, like the one shown above, should be replaced (See pages 60 to 61).

Repairing windows

"Windows" are actually three-part systems that add light and ventilation to your home. The parts are the window itself, the framing that surrounds the window and the trim, flashing and weatherstripping that seal the gaps between the window and framing and within the window itself.

Common problems that plague windows include broken glass, torn screening, damage to the sash frames that hold the glass or screening, and mechanical failure of the tracks and hardware that allow the window to operate. Framing problems, including rotted sills or rough sills and out-of-square framing members, are caused by moisture penetration or shifting of the house. Trim and weatherstripping fail from prolonged exposure to the elements—in most cases, it's easier and cheaper to replace failed weatherstripping or trim than to attempt to repair it.

Window problems can be found in just about every older home. Most window repair and weatherstripping products made and sold today are designed to correct problems that are unique to older style windows. Repairing older windows is comparatively easy, as long as you understand how the window works and have a realistic appreciation for when it's time to throw in the towel and replace the unit. Newer windows (those built and installed after 1980 or so) were designed to be "maintenance free," with integral weatherstripping, vinyl or metal cladding and multiple panes of energy-efficient window glass. When problems do occur in newer windows, most solutions involve replacing failed window parts, and the toughest part of the job may be disassembling the "sealed" window unit.

Specialty tools, like the window glazing knife shown above, can turn messy chores into quick and neat fixes.

Quick fixes for some common window problems

Problem: Aluminum sliding windows stick, bind or rock in frame.
Cure: Thoroughly clean the upper and lower frame rails with an abrasive pad, stiff bristle brush and all-purpose household cleaner. Vacuum up loose debris. Lubricate the channels with penetrating lubricant or silicone spray. In severe cases, you may need to remove the sash and replace worn plastic sash rollers and/or the vinyl jamb liner. Also check the channel flanges for dents that impair smooth operation. Remove dents by placing a wood block inside the channel and hammering the flange flat against the wood block.

Problem:: Frost or moisture condensation on interior side of window.
Cure: Add or replace weatherstripping around the window; install and insulate exterior storm windows. See pages 132 to 139 for more information on weatherizing.

Problem: Casement or awning window does not operate smoothly.
Cure: Clean and lubricate all moving parts. Use a wire brush or abrasive pad and all-purpose household cleaner to remove dirt, grime and grease from hinges, extension arm and track, and window operator. Lubricate the track, pivot points and operator gears with silicone spray.

Problem: Window operator is faulty (loose or broken crank, stripped or gummed-up gears, etc.).
Cure: Remove and replace the operator. To remove the operator from a casement window, fully open the window, then remove the screws that attach the operator to the window frame (on some models, the screws will be hidden under the bottom window stop, which must be removed to access them). Next, remove the screws or spring clips that hold the extension arm in the track. Pull the operator inward to remove. On awning windows, detach the scissor arms from the sash bracket and remove the operator as described above. If the operator is simply gummed up, soak it in kerosene or degreaser to remove grease and grime, lubricate with silicone spray, and reinstall. Damaged operators will need to be replaced, although finding an exact match may be tough. If this is the case, you may need to replace the entire assembly.

Common window types

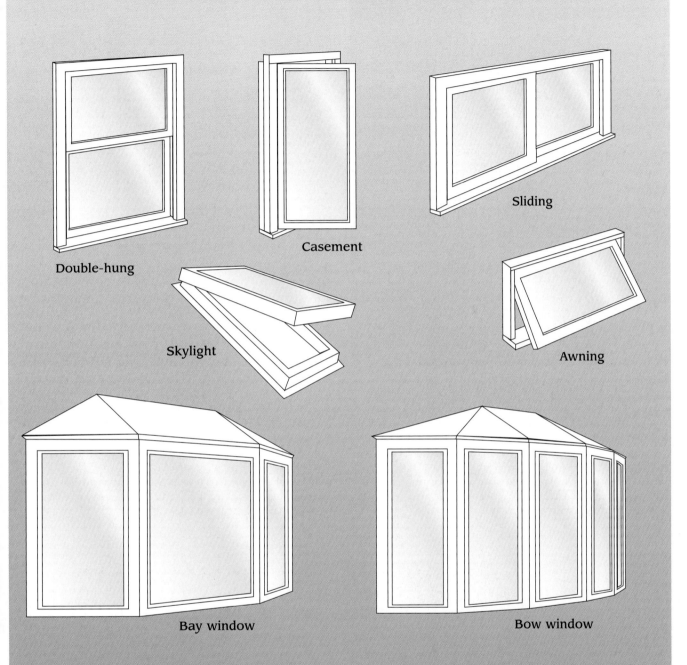

Double-hung

Casement

Sliding

Skylight

Awning

Bay window

Bow window

The simplest windows are fixed windows—they don't open or close, thus have no moving parts. Problems with such windows are typically restricted to broken glass, damage to exterior frames and loose or missing glazing.

The three most common operating window types include *double-hung windows, casement windows* and *sliding windows*. The frames and sashes may be wood, steel, aluminum or vinyl-clad, or any combination of these. Other less-common operating windows include *awning windows* (used mostly in basements) and *skylights*. Skylights, sometimes

called *roof windows*, can be operating or fixed. Repair and maintenance techniques are similar to casement and awning windows. Leaky skylights are often the result of flashing failure on the skylight curb (See *Roof Systems*, pages 99 to 109). *Bay windows* and *bow windows* are larger banks of windows that project from the house. The windows themselves are usually double-hung or casement style. Narrow side windows in bays and bows frequently are fixed. Leaks in bays and bows often result from shingle or flashing problems on the protective roof over the window bank (See pages 80 to 109).

Tips for making window repairs

Releasing sashes that are painted shut. Whether you need to make repairs or simply want to open a window and let the fresh air in, releasing window sashes that have been painted shut can be a real problem. A knife can be used to cut the window loose, but you risk damaging the jambs or the sash frame if the knife slips. The best tool to use for the job is the inexpensive *paint zipper* (available at hardware stores). Run the serrated blade of the zipper along the gap between the sash and the jambs and sill to break the paint seal. If the window still won't open, use a flat pry bar and wood block to pry the sash open from outside the house.

Removing interior casework. To remove a window sash frame for repair, you normally need to pry off the interior window trim first. Use a flat pry bar to remove the side trim pieces (you won't need to remove the top or bottom trim in most cases). Start prying near one end of each piece. A wood block inserted beneath the pry bar will increase your leverage and protect the wall surface. Pry only a little at a time to avoid damaging the trim, and work your way toward the other end of the trim piece. If you're working on more than one window, label the backs of the trim pieces so you know where they go when it's time to reinstall the trim.

Freeing-up sticky sashes

If your double-hung window sash is sticking in the window frame, correct the problem by thoroughly cleaning the side channels with a stiff brush and household cleaner. Vacuum up any loose debris. Scrape off paint and built-up grit with a paint scraper or sharp chisel. Lubricate the channels with paraffin wax or silicone spray. If the window binds against the stops, use a hammer and wood block to tap the stops outward, away from the center of the track (See photo, left). If a few light taps don't do the trick, remove and reset the stops to provide clearance. If the window is too loose or rattles, move the stops inward.

Similarly, a bowed jamb can often be knocked back into alignment with a hammer and wood block. If the sash slides freely after a few firm taps on the jamb, insert countersunk wood screws into the bowed section to secure it. If this doesn't work, you'll need to replace the jamb or lightly plane one side of the sash to fit.

How to repair deteriorated wood sash frames

1 Fill deteriorated areas of a wood window sash frame with exterior-rated wood filler product applied into a "form." Make the form from a thin strip of wood that is the same thickness as the rail or stile containing the damage. The strip should be a few inches longer than the damaged area. *TIP:* Lightly coat the inside surface of the strip with cooking spray so it will be easier to release the form when the filler dries. After cleaning the repair area with a stiff-bristled brush, attach the form to the sash frame rail or stile with masking tape (for large repair areas, drive a few finishing nails through the form and into the sash frame). Prepare and fill the damaged area with wood filler, following the instructions on the product container (See pages 58 to 59 for more information on using wood filler). Strike off the filler material with a broad putty knife riding along the top of the form and the rail or stile.

2 After the wood filler product has fully cured, remove the form from the sash frame. Use a hand-sanding block with 80- to 100-grit sandpaper to smooth the surfaces and edges of the repair area. Touch up with paint to match the rest of the sash frame and hide the repair.

How to repair wood sash frame corner joints

1 Remove the sash frame from the window. If the glass pane is still intact, chip off the dried glazing compound, pry out the glazier's points and carefully remove the glass. If only one corner joint is loose, scrape out as much of the dried glue from the joint as you can using a putty knife. Reglue and clamp the joint. Add reinforcement (wood screws or dowels) after the glue has dried. If the frame has two or more loose joints, break the joints apart and clean off dried glue with a scraper and sandpaper.

2 Apply moisture-resistant wood glue to the mating parts of each joint (a mortise-and-tenon joint is shown here). Clamp the frame together with pipe or bar clamps. Check to make sure the frame is square by measuring the diagonals, and adjust the clamps as needed until square is achieved. After clamping, clean off any glue squeeze-out with a damp rag. After the glue dries, reinforce the joint with dowels or grooved dowel pins inserted through guide holes drilled through the face of the joint. If the rails and stiles are connected with butt joints (not mortise-and-tenon joints), drill dowel holes through the side edge of the stile and about 1 in. into the rail. For mitered joints, drill dowel holes diagonally. Coat the dowels with glue before tapping them in place with a mallet or hammer. After the glue dries, use a backsaw or dovetail saw to cut the projecting dowel ends flush to the surface, then sand smooth.

How to repair a rotted window sill

Window sills are typically the first window frame component to show rot. The sill ends usually decay first due to trapped water between the sill and side frames. In severe cases, the side jambs, trim and stops, and bottom corners of the window sash will also be affected. Patch small holes, cracks and indentations with conventional wood filler. New latex fillers provide good adhesion and weather resistance combined with easy cleanup. To repair larger areas, use polyester resin wood filler or, for best results, two-part epoxy wood filler.

If the window sill is split, worn or rotted beyond the point of repair, replace it. You can purchase replacement sill stock at some lumberyards, or you can make your own new sill in your workshop (See pages 60 to 61).

1 Probe the decayed area with an awl or screwdriver to see how far the rot extends beyond the visibly damaged area. Also scrape off loose or blistered paint around the damage. Rot often spreads deeper into the wood than it appears. If the damage is extensive or affects parts of the sill that bear on the rough sill below or support the brickmold or casework, you should replace the sill (See pages 60 to 61).

2 Scrape out spongy or punky wood with a stiff putty knife or wood chisel. For best results, remove material until you reach sound wood. But since applying wood hardeners and sealing up the source of moisture penetration will neutralize the spreading the of the rot, you can get away with removing only the loose material, provided the material left in place is in fair condition.

3 Drill ¼-in.-dia. holes into the rotted area to create "tooth" for the wood filler product. In larger repair areas (more than ½ in. deep), drive galvanized deck screws into the wood, leaving the screw head protruding slightly, to help hold the filler. Apply liquid wood hardener (or the consolidant if using two-part epoxy wood filler) to the wood surface in and around the repair area.

4 Scuff up (scarify) any painted areas adjacent to the rotted section using 150-grit sandpaper to provide better adhesion for the wood filler. Make sure the repair area is clean and bone dry before applying the filler. Apply the wood filler, following the instructions on the product container. Press the filler firmly in place, roughly conforming it to the original shape of the damaged sill. If you've drilled bonding holes, force the product into the holes with a ¼-in. dowel until full.

5 Smooth and shape the filled section with a plastic putty knife while the filler is still soft. Before application, dip the knife in mineral spirits to prevent the filler from sticking to it. Take care not to strike off filler past the plane of the adjoining wood surfaces.

6 After the wood filler has fully cured, further shape the patch with a rasp or wood file. Either of these tools will remove excess filler more quickly than sanding and will not burnish the surface as over-sanding can. Clean the tool with a wire brush and solvent immediately after you're finished using it.

7 Hand-sand the finished profile onto the patch using 150-grit sand-paper with a sanding block or a medium-grit sanding sponge. Immediately coat the repaired area with matching exterior paint/primer or wood stain.

How to replace a window sill

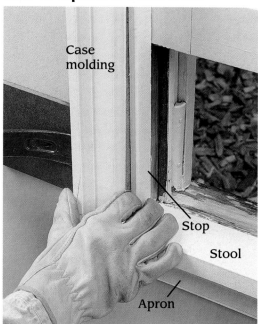

1 Remove the interior window case molding with a flat pry bar, then remove the apron molding, the stool and the stop molding. Use care to avoid damaging these parts so they may be reinstalled.

2 Measure and note the length of the existing sill. Cut through the sill on each end of a 1-ft.-wide section near the the center of the sill, using a reciprocating saw. Pry out the section.

Building a replacement window sill

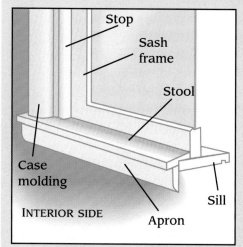

INTERIOR SIDE

The window sill creates a transition between the interior and exterior side of a window. Attached to the rough sill at the bottom of the framed opening, the sill is connected to the stool to create a stop for the window sash on the interior side. To replace a window sill, you normally need to remove the stool as well as the apron and case molding.

To build a replacement sill, measure the length of the existing sill before removal, then use a cross-section piece of the sill to find the width, thickness and bevel angles of the edges. Lay out the new sill on 2× stock, or

purchase premilled sill stock at your local lumberyard. The new sill should be long enough to provide for a sill horn that extends ½ to ¾ in. beyond the outside edges of the exterior window trim or brickmold. Measure, mark and cut notches in the sill ends with a jigsaw to form the sill horn (See photo above). Make sure the notches are deep enough so the inside edge of the sill and window jamb will be flush when the sill is installed. Test fit the sill and adjust as necessary.

3 Working from the exterior side, drive the cut end pieces inward with a hammer and wood block to remove them. If the pieces do not come out easily, split them lengthwise with a hammer and chisel, then free them from the side jambs. Remove or cut off any protruding nails from the side jambs and rough sill. Build or purchase a replacement sill (See previous page). Apply primer to the entire sill before installation.

4 Tack or staple two layers of building paper to the rough sill, allowing a slight overhang on both sides. Apply a wavy bead of construction adhesive to the building paper. Working from the outside, tap the new finish sill into place. *TIP:* For maximum protection against water damage, install a metal or plastic sill pan over the rough sill before installing the replacement sill (See page 72). Toenail the sill ends to the insides of the jambs with 8d galvanized casing nails. Then, drive galvanized 10d finish nails down through the sill and into the rough sill. Also drive nails up through the bottom of the sill horns and into the outside trim strips and jambs. Drill pilot holes in the horn areas to prevent splitting.

5 Reattach the stool, apron and stops. Set all nailheads with a nailset and cover the nail holes with exterior wood filler. Caulk all joints and gaps, then paint the sill (and trim pieces, if necessary).

A painter's tool (above) has a blade shaped like a slotted screwdriver head that is designed for setting glazier's points into a wood sash.

Replacing a window pane is relatively easy. Here, we'll show you how to replace single-pane glass in wood sash and metal sash windows. If the sash is hard to remove (which is often the case with old-style double-hung windows or casement windows), it's often easier to replace the glass with the sash in place. If the sash is easy to remove, you're better off taking it out and finishing the job on a flat surface.

Removing broken glass

Everyone agrees that handling broken glass should be done with great care, but you'll find quite a bit of disagreement on whether it's better to remove glass shards while the broken pane is still mounted in the window frame, or to remove the sash frame first, then extract the glass shards on a flat worksurface. Removing broken glass first minimizes the risk of accidents that can occur when removing a sash frame, but working on the window while in place is more awkward and gives less control over where the shards end up. If you're working on a sash frame that's still in place, apply masking tape over the broken pane to help hold the pieces together, and spread tarps on both sides of the window to catch the falling glass. You may even want to staple building paper or heavy plastic to the frame to catch the glass. **Always wear heavy work gloves, eye protection and a long-sleeved shirt when handling broken glass.**

Options for softening old glazing compound

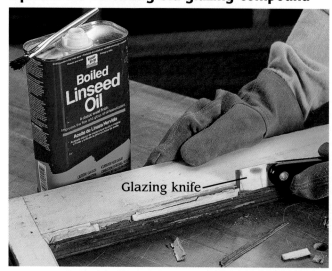

Glazing knife

Linseed oil. To soften old glazing compound and make it easier to remove with a glazing knife (top photo) or a putty knife, brush a coat of boiled linseed oil onto the compound a few hours before attempting to remove the glazing. This is the safest method for softening glazing compound.

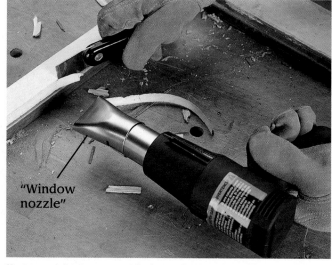

"Window nozzle"

Heat gun. A heat gun set at its lowest heat setting will also soften glazing compound and make it easier to remove. A slotted "window nozzle" attachment helps direct the hot air and keep it from igniting nearby paint chips and wood splinters. This is the fastest way to soften glazing compound. IMPORTANT: Linseed oil is flammable—do not use oil and a heat gun together!

How to replace glass in a wood sash frame

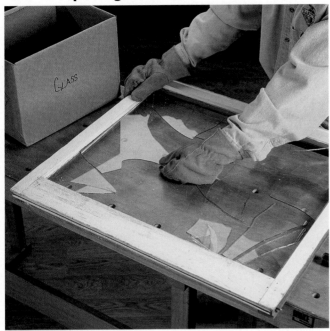

1 Remove the window sash frame containing the broken glass pane (See *page 56* and *Removing broken glass,* previous page). Remove all loose glass by grasping the shards firmly and rocking the pieces back and forth, then lifting them out of the frame (use pliers for small pieces). If you need to break the glass to remove it, tap the pane lightly with the end of an 8-ft. 2×4. Stand well clear of the window until the glass shatters. Deposit the shards immediately into a cardboard box or garbage can.

2 Remove old glazing compound from the frame (See *Options,* previous page). Pry out the glazier's points from the recess in the sash frame using a slotted screwdriver. Clean out the recess with a wire brush to remove all traces of the old glass, glazing compound or wood splinters. For ordering a new glass pane, measure the width and length of the opening, then subtract ⅛ in. from each dimension for expansion.

OPTION 1: GLAZING COMPOUND

OPTION 2: CAULK

3 Before installing the new glass, prepare the recess. To create a tight seal and prevent the glass from ratting in the frame, lay a bed of glazing compound or caulk. **Glazing compound (left photo):** If you're using glazing compound to make a bed for the glass pane, treat the recess with boiled linseed oil to improve the adhesion of the glazing compound. Then, roll the compound into thin coils or "ropes"

and lay the ropes onto the ledge of the recess. Set the ropes in place by pressing down on them lightly with a putty knife or glazing tool coated with linseed oil. **Caulk (right photo):** A bead of caulk (silicone is best, but latex or acrylic-based also will work) laid on the recess is faster to apply than glazing compound and accomplishes essentially the same results. (Continued on next page)

How to replace glass in a wood sash frame (continued)

4 Wearing gloves, set the new glass pane in the recess so the gap is even on all sides. Lightly press it into the bed of caulk or glazing compound. With a screwdriver or painter's tool (See page 62), press glazier's points into the sash frame every 6 to 8 in. to hold the glass pane in place.

5 Roll glazing compound into ropes about ½ in. in dia. and place the ropes around the perimeter of the exterior side of the glass, making sure the glazier's points are covered. Smooth and bevel the glazing compound with a stiff metal putty knife or a glazing knife held at a 45° angle to the sash. Lubricate the knife blade with linseed oil to keep the compound from lifting or stretching along the bead or sticking to the knife. Squeezed-out compound on either side of the bead can be removed with a razor blade after the compound dries.

Other options for glazing a window

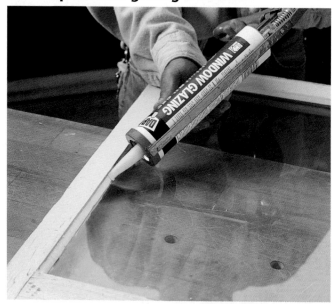

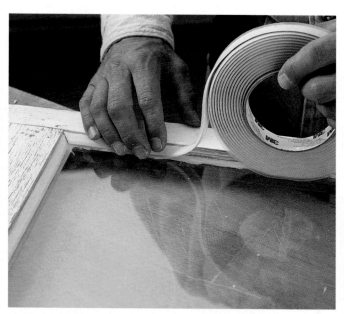

Instead of standard glazing compound, there are a couple of options for applying window glazing that are worth considering (deciding which to use is purely a matter of personal choice). *Cartridge-style window glazing* (left photo): This product is especially popular with handymen who are well-versed in handling a caulk gun. The tube cartridges fit into a caulk gun as caulk cartridges do, and their use can greatly reduce the amount of time it takes to glaze a window or windows. The trick is to make sure you trim off the tip of the cartridge

nozzle so the sides are at a 45° angle and the top of the cutoff line is flat. If you maintain a steady pace, you may get a smooth enough bead that you don't even need to go back and strike off the glazing material with a putty knife. *Glazing tape* (right photo): This easy-to-use product is simply pre-shaped glazing compound with attached backing that is sold in rolls. To apply it, you roll it out, press the tape into place, then remove the backing. While it is virtually foolproof to apply, it is more expensive than other glazing options.

How to replace glass in a metal sash frame

Unlike wood window sash frames, which are all fairly similar in construction, metal sash frames have been made using a host of different types of joinery. And even frames with similar frame joinery often employ entirely different methods to hold the glass panes into the frame. Regardless of the metal frame type, the sequence for replacing glass can be boiled down to disassembling the frame, replacing the glass, then reassembling the frame around the new glass.

Some older steel and aluminum windows have panes set in glazing compound. For this type, glass replacement is essentially the same as for wood-sash windows, except that the pane is held in place with metal spring clips instead of glazier's points. After removing the old compound, remove the old clips by pinching them and pulling them out of the sash.

Another type of metal window (usually with double insulated panes) has beveled, snap-out "hard" vinyl moldings. After removing the broken glass, pry up one end of each strip with a putty knife, and pull them out by hand to access the pane. After installing the new pane, snap the strips back in place by hand. Glass in most metal frames with corner connectors (also called *keys*) and rubber gaskets is replaced more or less in keeping with the sequence shown here.

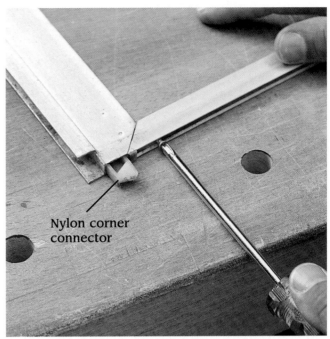

Nylon corner connector

1 After removing the sash frame (See *Removing broken glass*, page 62), disassemble the frame at the corners. Metal sash frames employ a wide variety of connection methods to make the corner joints. The frame shown above is held together with L-shaped nylon corner brackets that are secured with set screws. To disassemble, simply remove the set screws on adjacent corners and pull the frame apart. If the corner connectors are held in place by crimping, drill out the crimped portion of the frame. See *NOTE*, Step 3.

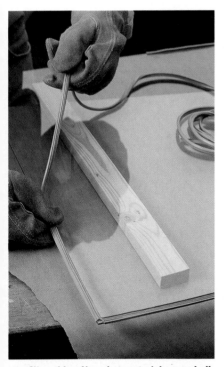

2 Slip rubber U-gasket material around all edges of the new glass pane. Make a slit in the outer edge of the gasket at each corner so the material will make the corner without buckling.

3 Reassemble the metal frame around the new glass pane, making sure the rubber gasket fits snugly into the inner channels of the frame pieces. If the corner connectors are still in good condition, re-use them. If not, bring one of the old connectors to a hardware store that repairs storm windows and purchase matching replacements. *NOTE:* Because there are so many types of corner connectors used in metal sash frames, make sure you can find replacement connectors (or plan on re-using the old ones) before purchasing the new window glass.

Aluminum

Fiberglass

Replacement window screening is generally made from aluminum or fiberglass. Traditional steel screening is seldom found used anymore to its tendency to rust. Fiberglass screening is easier to handle and generally will create a better match with nearby windows that don't have new screening. Aluminum screening is more durable. Screening is usually sold in rolls with widths that match standard window sizes. Be sure to allow for trim waste when purchasing screening.

Replacing window screening

Holes or rips in screens signal an open invitation for flies, mosquitoes and other pests to invade the house. While temporary patches can provide immediate relief, they're unsightly, and usually not worth the hassle. In the long run, it's better to replace the screening. The tools and materials needed for the job are quite inexpensive.

Replace all window and door screening on a flat worksurface, not with the frame mounted in the window. Some repair procedures require you to manipulate the screen frames to create tension in the screening—a necessary ingredient to obtaining a ripple-free screen that does not sag.

Removable screen windows are especially vulnerable to damage during transportation or storage. To reduce the risk, store screen windows off the ground and in a remote corner of your garage or basement while the glass storm windows are in place. Regular cleaning with a brush, detergent and garden hose also helps prolong the life of screen windows.

Screen retainer strips

Screening is held in wood sash frames with staples that are concealed by thin wood retainer strips. Because they are so thin, retainer strips are highly susceptible to splitting and to wood rot. Unless the retainer strips on your window are in excellent condition, it's a good idea to replace them at the same time you replace the screening. Most building centers carry retainer strip molding in the most common profiles (See photo, right). To prevent deterioration, prime and paint all sides of the new strips before installing your new screening. Also, prevent splitting and cracking by drilling pilot holes for the galvanized wire brads used to attach the retainer strips to the wood frame.

Temporary screen repairs

While replacing damaged screening is always a better idea than trying to patch holes or tears, you may not be able to get to the project right away. To keep insects out of your home until the screening is properly replaced, try these quick fixes:

Aluminum or steel screening: If you've got some extra screening lying around, cut a patch slightly larger than the damaged area, then unravel the cross-woven strands on each side to expose about ¼ in. of each strand. Position the patch over the damage and weave the exposed wire into the original screening. If you don't have extra screening material, mend the damaged area with a sewing needle and fishing line.

Fiberglass or plastic screening: Use rubber cement to glue rips together or attach small patches over the damaged area. Use tape to hold the torn screening together or to temporarily hold the patch in place, while the cement is applied. Rips also can be sewn shut.

How to replace screening in a metal frame

Spline cord

1 Pull out the rubber spline cord at one corner of the frame, using a slotted screwdriver or awl to get the cord started. Once the spline cord is removed, the old screening should fall out or lift out easily. Clean out the spline cord channel with a stiff brush and household cleaner.

2 Place the screen frame on a flat work surface, making sure the frame is square. Lay the new screening material over the frame—there should be an overlap of at least 1 in. on all sides. To prevent the screening from kinking, trim off the corners, leaving some overlapping material.

3 Starting at the bottom of the screen, secure the new screening in the spline channel by pressing new spline cord into the channel with a spline roller. Do not re-use the old spline cord. Work your way around the screen frame, without cutting the spline cord. If necessary, force the spline cord into the corners with a screwdriver. Maintain a small amount of tension in the screen when securing the final two sides, but don't tug too hard on it, or the frame may bow inward.

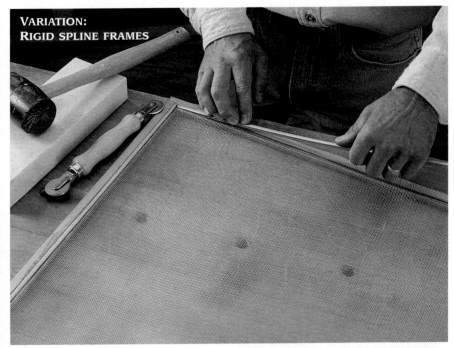

VARIATION: RIGID SPLINE FRAMES

VARIATION: Rigid spline frames. Some older metal screen frames don't rely on rubber spline cord to hold the screening; instead they use rigid metal rods that are driven over the screening and into the spline channels. If you have this type of screen frame, lay the new screen material in place, then force each edge into the spline channel with a spline roller. Position the rigid spline and press it into the channel. If you're having difficulty seating the spline in the channel, rap it gently with a mallet and a wood block.

4 Once the new screening is secured, check to make sure there are no ripples and that the pattern of the screening is square to the frame. If not, remove the spline cord, make adjustments, then reinstall the cord. Trim off excess screening with a utility knife.

How to replace screening in a wood frame

1 First, cut any paint seal between the retainer strip molding and the frame using a sharp utility knife. Then, pry off the retainer strips using a small pry bar or a wood chisel with the flat side facing up. Pull out brads or staples from the retainer strip and wood frame, using locking pliers. Inspect the retainer strips—if they're not in excellent condition, replace them with new strips (See page 66).

2 Lay new screening over the frame and secure the frame to your worksurface with clamps. The replacement screening should overhang the outer edges of the frame by at least 1 in. at the ends (unless you're using fiberglass screening, which only needs to overlap the inside edges of the frame opening by an inch or so per side). Adjust the screening so the perpendicular cross-hatch pattern of the material is square to the frame. Fasten the screening at the top or bottom of the frame by driving staples into the frame or frame channel. Keep the staples contained within the area that was covered by the retainer strips. When stapling, drive the staples at a slight angle to catch two or more strands of screening.

VARIATION: FIBERGLASS SCREENING

VARIATION: Fiberglass screening. If installing fiberglass screening, fold the end of the material back over itself before stapling to form a double-layer hem that will better resist tearing as the material is stretched.

3 Stretch the screening tight and staple it to the opposite end of the frame in the same manner. If you're replacing a screen in a screen door or very long window, staple the free end of the screening to a piece of scrap wood and pull on the scrap to draw the screening taut, then staple it down.

4 Staple down one side, then pull the screening taut to the other side. Take care not to create uneven pressure (you'll see a waviness in the screening pattern if the pressure is uneven). Staple down the screening on the second side. Inspect the results and, if you're not completely happy with the outcome, try again. It's not uncommon, even for experienced handymen, to take a few attempts at new screen installation before getting it right.

5 Reattach the screen retainer strip molding over the edges of the screening, using 1-in. wire brads spaced 8 to 10 in. apart. Use needle-nose pliers or a thin strip of scrap to hold the brads while you hammer them in place. If reusing the old retainer strips, don't use the old nail holes. Trim off excess screening with a utility knife. For the cleanest look, set the nailheads, cover them with exterior wood filler, then touch up or repaint the frame. Or, save a little time and effort by simply painting over the heads of the brads.

After weatherstripping and hardware, the framing surrounding exterior doors is the most vulnerable part of a door "system." But because the structural elements beneath the door generally are hidden by siding and steps, we often don't realize that repairs are needed until it's too late—as with the entry door above. Here, the only alternative is to replace the rotted rim joist and mud sill, as well as the worn threshold.

Exterior doors that are well maintained and well made to begin with can last as long as any other part of your home. But more often than not, entry doors, side doors, service doors and garage doors fail prematurely and require replacement.

The greatest favor you can do for any exterior door is to install a storm door that will bear the brunt of the exposure. A good storm door also will help reduce energy costs and allow you to increase ventilation.

Adequate weatherstripping and a good threshold seal are also important to prolonging the life of a door, as well as reducing air transfer and eliminating pest entry points. And as with any part of your home that is made of wood, door frames, sills and wood thresholds are subject to rot and infestation and need to be monitored regularly.

Garage doors are sometimes overlooked when it comes to door maintenance, but because of their size, weight and complex opening mechanisms, they should be included in all routine maintenance exercises.

How to patch a section of a rim joist

1 Once you have identified that a section of rim joist is in need of replacement, peel back siding and other obstructions so you can inspect the adjoining sections of the joist. Replace joist lumber until you reach undamaged wood. In the structural situation shown above, the rim joist is not bearing significant weight—partly because it's in such poor condition. If your rim joist is bearing structural weight, you'll need to shore up the adjoining joists from below (the basement or crawlspace) to take on the load while the new joist section is installed. Make a straight cut at the ends of the damaged area, then pry out the deteriorated joist material with a wrecking bar.

Furring

2 Cut a replacement section of material to length from 2× stock the same width as the existing rim joist (on older homes, you may need to rip-cut the wood to match the old joists). Attach the new rim joist. In the situation shown above, the void between the rim joist and the next floor joist was filled with concrete. 2× blocking between the joists was installed to create nailing surfaces. The new section was attached with 16d galvanized common nails. A strip of ¾-in. treated lumber was tacked to the face of the new joist to bring it flush with the adjoining furring strips, then new building paper was attached and the siding was replaced in the repair area.

How to replace a door sill & threshold

1 If both the threshold and sill require replacement, start by removing the old threshold. First, cut it in half with a back saw, being careful not to damage the interior flooring. Starting at the center, pry up each threshold section, removing nails as you go. When both sections are loosened, twist the pieces from side to side, pulling outward to free the ends from beneath the door jambs. If a section won't come out easily, make a second cut 3 to 4 in. away from the jamb and split the end into several pieces with a chisel. Pull or clip off any protruding nails in the jamb and sill.

2 Remove the door sill in much the same way as you would remove a window sill (See pages 60 to 61). Cut out a section of the sill with a reciprocating saw, pry the section loose, then pry out the ends of the threshold, splitting them, if necessary, with a wood chisel. Try to keep as much of the old threshold intact as you can to provide a template for cutting a replacement threshold.

2×2 nailer

3 *TIP:* If the sill location falls over a void between the outer and inner rim joists, attach cleats or nailers to the existing framework to create a stable nailing surface for attaching the back edge of the new sill.

(Continued on next page)

How to replace a door sill & threshold (continued)

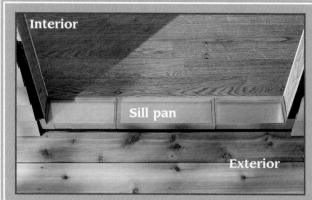

OPTION: Install a sill pan. After removing the old sill, install a plastic or metal sill pan to help prevent future water or termite damage. The back edge and ends of a sill pan extend up above sill height, while the front edge extends down over the rim joist or wall sheathing. Install the sill pan following manufacturer's instructions (the adjustable sill pan shown here is bonded to the mud sill with construction adhesive and nailed to the door opening framing members). You can buy sill pans at building centers or have one custom-made by a sheet-metal fabricator.

4 Cut the new sill to length (width of the opening minus ⅛ in.). The width and thickness should match the old sill. If the old sill was beveled at the edges, cut matching bevels with a circular saw and straightedge. Cut notches to create "horns" that match the old sill.

5 Prime the new sill, then attach it to the mud sill with 16d galvanized finish nails (drill pilot holes for the nails near the horns to prevent the wood from splitting). Where possible, position the nails so they will be hidden by the threshold. Set nailheads, then fill the nail holes with caulk. Caulk any gaps around the sill.

6 Reinstall or replace the threshold with a new unit (See *Threshold types,* below). If necessary, trim the bottoms of the door jambs and stops to accommodate the new threshold. Adjust threshold height according to the manufacturer's directions. *NOTE:* Most new thresholds contain an adjustment screw for easy adjustments (See inset photo).

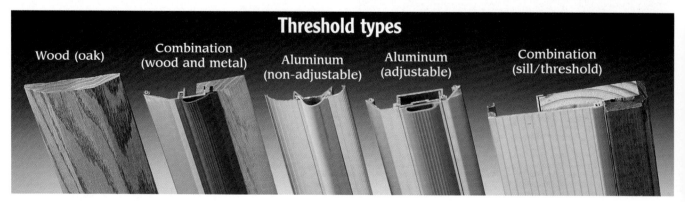

Threshold types

Wood (oak)   Combination (wood and metal)   Aluminum (non-adjustable)   Aluminum (adjustable)   Combination (sill/threshold)

How to replace brick molding

Brick molding is the trim, usually profiled, that surrounds a door or window on the exterior side (despite the name, it is found on homes with just about every type of siding). The brick molding generally fits between the door or window frame and siding, which butts up against the outer edges of the molding pieces. Drip edge flashing fits over the top piece of brick molding and is slipped beneath the siding above the door or window opening. Damage occurs most frequently on the top section, especially at the mitered corners.

1 Pry off the damaged brick molding with a flat pry bar. Repair any siding damage behind the trim (See pages 34 to 49). Also replace any deteriorated building paper.

2 Cut a piece of new brick molding (the new stock should have the same thickness, width and profile) slightly longer than the damaged piece. Hold the molding upside-down over the repair area and transfer cutting marks for the outsides of the miters. Cut to size and test-fit the replacement piece.

3 If you're replacing the top piece of molding, also replace the old drip edge flashing (if present) with a new piece of drip edge. You can usually find an exact match at a hardware store or lumberyard. Slip the drip edge between the siding and building paper, and caulk around the joints. You don't need to nail the drip edge—the brick molding will hold it in place. If the door or window does not have a drip edge, you can install one.

4 Miter-cut new brick molding pieces, prime and paint them to match, and nail them to door or window framing with 16d galvanized casing nails. Apply a bead of construction adhesive to one of the mating ends before making each joint. Lock-nail the miter joints between the side and top pieces of brickmold using 8d galvanized finish nails. Attach molding to the door header and side jambs by applying a bead of construction adhesive to the backside of the molding, then pressing the molding in place. Set the nailheads and fill the nail holes with exterior wood filler.

Sliding doors

Most sliding patio doors provide years of trouble-free service, requiring little more than a periodic cleaning of the track on which they ride and occasional cleaning, lubing and adjustment of the rollers to keep them running smoothly. But over time, the rollers will wear, causing them to drag, jump off the track or not hold their adjustment, and will need to be replaced.

Sliding door rollers

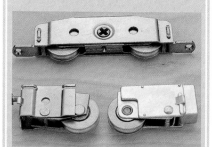

Common styles of replacement rollers.

If cleaning, adjustment and lubrication of the rollers and tracks don't correct a problem with a poorly operating sliding door, the chances are good that the rollers require replacement. To access the rollers, remove the door and lay it across two padded sawhorses.

On many newer doors, you can simply pry out the roller with a screwdriver. On older doors, you may have to disconnect the stile from the bottom rail, then slide the roller out from the end. On these, the same screw that connects the rail to the stile also holds the roller in place.

Bring the old rollers to a glass repair shop to find replacements (always replace rollers in pairs). If the shop doesn't have the model you need in stock, they may be able to order it for you, especially if you can identify the door manufacturer. To install the new rollers, simply reverse the sequence you used to remove the old ones. Adjust as needed after the door is reinstalled.

Tips for maintaining sliding doors

Clean the track. Clean the tracks and jambs with household cleaner and an abrasive scouring pad or stiff bristle brush. Remove corrosion and small nicks or dings on the track rails with 220-grit "wet-or-dry" silicon-carbide paper. Minor bends or dings in the track can be bent back into shape with padded locking pliers. (A few wraps of masking tape around the toothed jaws will prevent damage to the rail.) A light coat of paraffin wax on the rails will make for smooth, quiet operation.

Adjust the rollers. Most sliding door rollers adjust by means of a height adjustment screw, accessed by a hole in the face or end of the door at each roller location. Generally, you don't need to remove the door to adjust the rollers. Simply turn the adjustment screw one way or the other until the bottom edge of the door is parallel with the track and the latch side fits flush against the side jamb. Also, make sure the latch mechanism aligns with the catch in the side jamb and that the door glides smoothly.

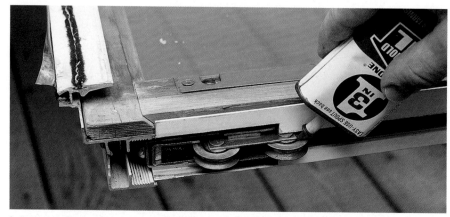

Lubricate rollers with machine oil or silicone lubricant. Do not apply lubricant to the track or the door threshold.

Garage door opening systems

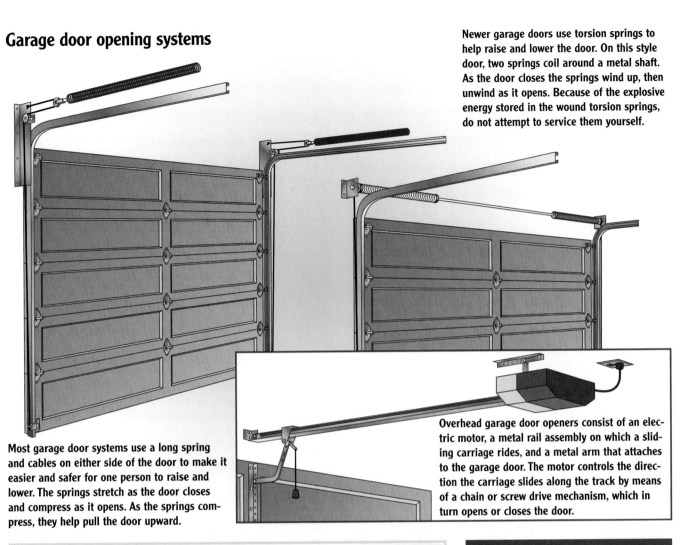

Newer garage doors use torsion springs to help raise and lower the door. On this style door, two springs coil around a metal shaft. As the door closes the springs wind up, then unwind as it opens. Because of the explosive energy stored in the wound torsion springs, do not attempt to service them yourself.

Most garage door systems use a long spring and cables on either side of the door to make it easier and safer for one person to raise and lower. The springs stretch as the door closes and compress as it opens. As the springs compress, they help pull the door upward.

Overhead garage door openers consist of an electric motor, a metal rail assembly on which a sliding carriage rides, and a metal arm that attaches to the garage door. The motor controls the direction the carriage slides along the track by means of a chain or screw drive mechanism, which in turn opens or closes the door.

Garage door lubrication points

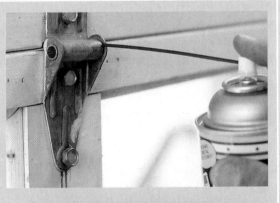

1 Lubricate pivot points on the hinges of sectional garage doors with silicone-based spray lubricant. Lubrication will prolong the life of the hinges and eliminate squeaking and creaking when the door opens and closes.

2 While you're at it, spray lubricant into the hinge rollers that ride in the metal door tracks to keep them rolling smoothly. Do not use oil or grease as a lubricant; heavy petroleum lubricants will attract dust and grit and damage the rollers.

Garage doors

Garage doors and door jambs take a beating from continual use and water damage, usually along the bottom edges where they come into contact with the concrete garage slab. Protect the garage door and jamb from the elements by keeping paint, caulking and weatherstripping in good repair. When rot does develop, repair or replace damaged areas to keep the rot from spreading.

Continual use, condensation, temperature extremes and dirt also are hard on garage door hardware and electric door openers. Clean and lubricate moving door parts, such as metal hinges and rollers, annually. If you need to replace your electric door opener, see the removal and replacement sequence shown on pages 77-79.

Rotten door jamb repair

1 Remove loose, punky rotted wood and blistered or peeling paint with a metal-bristle brush and paint scraper. Remove enough rotten wood to get down to a relatively sound base layer. Treat the repair area with liquid wood hardener (See page 58 for repairing a rotted window sill) and allow the jamb to dry thoroughly.

2 Spread exterior-grade wood filler over the repair area with a wide blade putty knife, overfilling the area slightly to allow for shrinkage. Let the filler dry. Flatten the jamb repair area with a rasp and file and smooth with 150-grit sandpaper. Then prime and paint the jamb with exterior-grade paint.

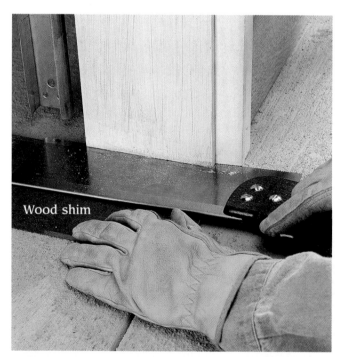

Wood shim

3 To keep the jamb from absorbing water off the concrete garage floor, remove the first ¼ in. of jamb with a backsaw. Use a ¼-in. wood shim beneath the saw blade to guide the blade and keep the saw cut even across the jamb bottom.

4 Fill the gap between the jamb bottom and the garage floor with a bead of caulk.

How to install a new garage door opener

1 Assemble the garage door opener rail sections on a flat surface and attach the sliding carriage mechanism to the rail assembly. Fasten the rail assembly to the garage door opener motor unit, according to the instructions supplied with the opener.

2 Unplug the old garage door opener from its power source and remove it. In this example, the opener mounted directly to the wallboard ceiling. If yours is suspended from roof trusses with brackets, you may be able to use the same brackets to hang the new opener. Verify this possibility with the instruction manual.

3 Determine the height of the rail assembly header bracket by raising the door to its highest position on the track. Measure from the top edge of the door to the floor and add 2½ in. to this distance. Lower the door. Mark the header bracket height on the wall above the garage door. Determine the center of the door and mark a centerline on the wall as well.

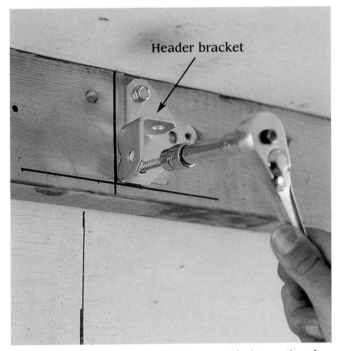

Header bracket

4 Install the header bracket with lag screws at the intersection of the two lines you determined in Step 3. The header bracket must be attached to solid framing, not to wallboard, particleboard or plywood alone. If the header bracket location does not fall on solid framing, position a piece of framing lumber over the wall sheathing and fasten it to the wall studs (as we show here) to serve as a header.

How to install a new garage door opener (continued)

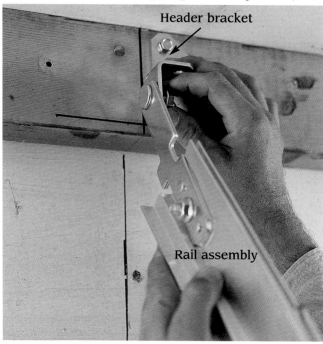

5 Connect the garage door opener rail assembly and motor unit to the header bracket. Pivot the rail assembly and motor unit up until the rail assembly is level with the header bracket. Position a step ladder underneath the motor unit to support the motor during this step. Slowly raise and lower the door by hand to be sure the rail assembly does not interfere with the door travel.

6 Attach the motor unit to the garage ceiling or roof trusses. Since garage ceiling fastening situations will vary, you'll need to modify your installation based on the ceiling you have. We attached 2×4s to the roof trusses, driving 3-in. deck screws through the 2×4s and wallboard and into the trusses. If the trusses are exposed, you can attach the motor with metal straps supplied with the opener.

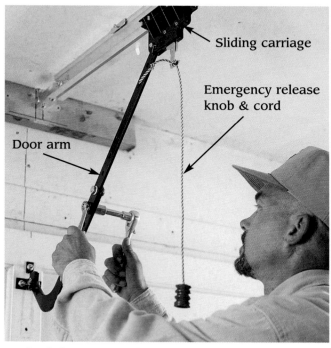

7 Find the centerpoint of the door and mark a line at the top. Center the door bracket on this line and position it near the top of the door so it rests on solid door framing. For doors without solid wood framing (such as those made of masonite, fiberglass or sheet metal), contact the door manufacturer for instructions on how to properly brace the area behind the door bracket. Bolt the bracket to the door.

8 Attach the emergency release knob and cord to the sliding carriage so the knob hangs 6 ft. from the floor. Assemble the curved and straight sections of the metal door arm with bolts so the arm is long enough to extend from the sliding carriage to the door bracket. Attach the door arm to the door bracket and sliding carriage.

9 Safety codes now require new garage door openers to be outfitted with motion sensors that reverse the path of the door when an object crosses their path. The sensors on the opener we installed fasten next to the garage door tracks near the floor, one on either side of the door. Follow the instructions that come with the opener for details on positioning and adjusting the sensors. Route and staple low-voltage electrical wire that comes with the opener from the sensors to the motor unit, being careful to keep the wires clear of moving door parts.

10 Locate wall controls for the opener within sight of the garage door and at least 5 ft. from the floor so children cannot reach them. Run wire from the wall controls to the motor unit. Use care when stapling the wire in place to keep from nicking it.

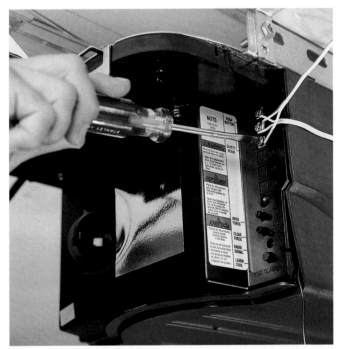

11 Attach the wiring from the wall controls and motion sensors to the appropriate motor unit terminals. *CAUTION: Be sure the motor is unplugged before you make these wiring connections.* Carefully strip ½ in. of insulation from the end of each wire lead and wrap the bare wire clockwise around the terminal post. Tighten the terminals snugly, but not so tight as to damage the wire.

12 Plug in the motor unit and test the garage door opener operation. You'll need to follow the instruction manual that comes with the opener to properly set the maximum up and down travel of the door. You'll also need to set the minimum force required to reverse the door when it meets an obstruction (like the 2×4 in the photo). The door should immediately stop and reverse.

Repairing Roof Systems

Your roof system is similar to a machine. It's composed of several different parts that work simultaneously for a single purpose: to protect your home from the elements. When one part breaks down it has a direct effect on the other parts and the net result is that the machine ceases to function at peak efficiency.

The principal parts of a roof system are the roof covering (the shingles, building paper and decking); the flashing that seals gaps around roof elements; the gutters and downspouts that direct water away from the roof and your house; the soffits and fascia that close in the eave area and improve the appearance of the roof; and the various vents and vent covers that comprise the ventilation system.

This chapter covers basic repairs you can make to each of these elements of the roof system to prevent further damage to the roof and house structure beneath.

With roof systems, as with most parts of your house, it makes little sense to take on repair projects until you've determined why the problem occurred. More often than not, some form of moisture is the culprit. Moisture can infect your roof system through failed flashings, damaged shingle areas or clogged gutters and downspouts. Or, it can develop inside the roof due to poor ventilation or vapor barrier and insulation problems.

If you discover a leak or any type of moisture problem, take immediate measures to seal off the leak and prevent additional damage from occurring. That may mean tacking a tarp over a shingle problem, slathering roof cement over a section of disconnected flashing, or simply positioning a bucket beneath

Parts of a Roof System

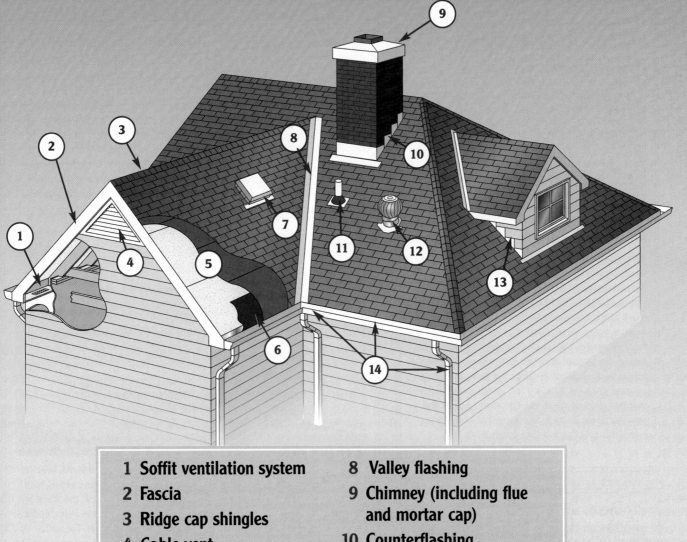

1 Soffit ventilation system	8 Valley flashing
2 Fascia	9 Chimney (including flue and mortar cap)
3 Ridge cap shingles	
4 Gable vent	10 Counterflashing
5 Roof covering (decking, building paper, shingles)	11 DWV stack with boot
	12 Turbine style roof vent
6 Ice guard underlayment	13 Step flashing
7 Flat roof vent	14 Gutter/downspout system

a leak to keep water from damaging surfaces or getting into structural areas of the house.

Then, do some investigating (you'll find plenty of tips in this section to help you trace leaks and identify problems). Once you've discovered why the problem exists, correcting it can be very easy (of course, it can also be a major headache). After the problem is addressed, go after the effects by replacing shingles, flashings or any other parts of the roof system that were damaged as a result of the problem.

Finally, set up a regular inspection and maintenance schedule for the roof system, as you should for other areas of the house (See pages 156 to 157). With roofs, the best times to inspect are in the fall (to seal up for winter) and in the spring (to assess any damage that may have occurred over winter). Depending on the size and shape of your house, you may not even need to get up onto the roof to perform an inspection. Often, simply walking around the house and observing with binoculars is enough to spot potential problems.

Problem: Damaged, worn or poorly installed shingles

Damaged, worn or poorly installed shingles should be replaced as soon as you notice them. As a roof ages, the mineral surfaces on asphalt and fiberglass composition shingles wear off, leaving the shingles more brittle and prone to damage. One early sign of wear is a large accumulation of granules in the gutters, so you can expect more problems in the near future. Pay special attention to the sunny side of the house, as sunlight compounds the damage caused by wind and rain. If only a few shingles or localized sections show damage, you can easily make repairs yourself; if the damage is widespread, plan on a complete reroofing job (See pages 87 to 93).

Problem: Missing shingles

Missing shingles should be replaced immediately. Shingles at the ridge and eave areas are generally the first to go, whether from excessive wear that weakens the shingles and causes them to become brittle, or from wind or other damage-causing forces. If excessive wear was the cause of the lost shingles, you're likely going to need to reroof your home in the near future. A few shingles blown off in a storm can be replaced and your roof should be as good as new (See pages 87 to 89).

Problem: Buckled shingles

Buckling and cupping result from moisture trapped beneath the shingles, which causes uneven drying. This problem is especially common on low-pitched roofs with slow drainage. Buckled asphalt shingles may flatten out after the source of moisture is removed. If not, either tack them back down with roof cement or replace them (See page 89). Cupped shingles should be replaced to prevent further damage from wind-driven rain.

Problem: Leaky gutters

Leaky gutter. Check gutter joints and connections for signs of leaks. Leaking joints in gutters and downspouts usually can be disassembled, caulked with gutter lap seal, then reassembled. Also, get up on a ladder and check inside the gutter for signs of rust and corrosion. Several products are available for resurfacing the insides of gutters and patching localized holes. For more severe damage, cut and install a short replacement pieces of gutter material, or replace the entire section (See pages 110 to 116).

Problem: Sagging gutters

Sagging gutters. A gutter system relies on gravity to work: When installed, all sections of gutter slope toward the nearest downspout location. But if a downspout becomes clogged, the weight of the trapped water can cause the gutters to sag, disrupting the flow of water. As the sag worsens, the stress increases. Clear blocked downspouts (See page 117), check for failed fasteners or damaged fascia, then rehang the gutters to reestablish the all-important slope (See page 111).

Problem: Disconnected gutters & downspouts

Disconnected downspout. Heavy rainstorms, strong winds, freezing and thawing, even a jolt from below can cause downspouts to become detached, either within the downspout run or at the connection to the gutters. This, of course, renders the downspout and gutter system useless. How the connection is reestablished depends on the type of gutter and downspout material. The metal downspout shown above should be reassembled with gutter lap sealant and pop rivets (See page 117).

Problem: Damaged flashing

Damaged flashing. Check flashings for rust or other forms of damage and deterioration, including tears or holes. If you notice minor surface rust or corrosion, sand and repaint with rust-resistant paint. You can sometimes extend the life of damaged flashings by coating them with a fibered roof cement, but plan on replacing the flashing within a few years (See pages 98 to 109).

Problem: Loose flashing

Loose flashing. While flashings often outlast the shingles, the roof cement or caulk used to seal them has a tendency to fail long before the flashing itself needs replacement. You may have to go up on the roof to detect minor cracks or holes in the sealant. As long as the flashing is in reasonably good shape, you can usually repair loose flashing by recaulking or replacing the old, brittle roof cement (See pages 98 to 109).

Problem: Soffit/eave damage

Rotted soffits. Check for signs of rot and water damage. Rotted or deteriorating soffits are often a result of inadequate attic ventilation—paint peeling off soffits is an early sign of this. Also check for pest damage. For information on repairing or adding soffits, see pages 118 to 121.

Problem: Rotted fascia

Rotted fascia. Fascia boards are subjected to considerable exposure to the elements, especially if adjoining parts of the roof system are in poor repair (like the shingles in the photo above). Pay special attention to fascia boards behind gutters, especially at joints and hanger locations. Correct the source of the problem then replace the fascia (See page 122).

Continued Next Page

Problem: Roof/wall separation

Separation can occur between any two parts of a roof system, causing a domino-effect of damage. In the photo above, a poor seal between the shingles and the dormer siding has led to serious rot near the roof edge. To repair the problem, the brittle roof-cement seal needs to be replaced with step flashing (See pages 106 to 107). Then, the rotted boards can be replaced (See pages 36 to 37).

Problem: Ice dams/poor roof ventilation

Ice dams form on roof eaves with inadequate attic ventilation. In addition to stressing the gutter systems, ice dams can cause interior leaking as the water backs up and works its way under the lower shingles (See pages 130 to 131). Improved ventilation (See pages 123 to 129) and a course or two of fully-bonded ice-guard membrane at the lower edge of the roof will solve the problem (although the bad news is that it's virtually impossible to replace building paper with ice guard without a total re-roofing project).

Tracking roof leaks

When you first notice a roof leak, arm yourself with a strong flashlight and visit your attic. First, check the roof area directly above the damp or dripping spot on the wall or ceiling. In most cases, you'll notice the origin of the leak will be higher up on the roof. During dry weather, look for water stains, streaks or rot on rafters and sheathing and follow them uphill to the highest point. If you can't get up on the roof to fix the problem immediately, mark the spot for future reference.

Inspect areas where pipes or vents penetrate the roof. Water stains here often indicate missing, damaged or improperly caulked vent or pipe flashings. If the flashing appears sound, but you still notice water stains where vent pipes or soil stacks penetrate the ceiling, the problem could be caused by moisture condensation due to poor roof ventilation or improperly installed attic insulation. Also inspect the roof framing and sheathing where the roof meets the exterior walls, along valleys and where dormers or chimneys penetrate the roof. Leaks or stains here usually indicate damaged or improperly sealed flashings. Water stains or rot at the low end of the roof, or on the interior of walls beneath, may result from ice dams or overflowing gutters. Conversely, stains near or along the ridge board generally indicate loose, cracked or missing ridge cap shingles. During your inspection, don't overlook holes from nails, staples or lag screws (such as TV antenna bolts), or similar small holes in the sheathing.

Roof repair materials

Roof cement is the glue that holds most roof repairs together. Known by many names in the building trades (including "Blackjack" after a popular brand of roof cement), it is sold in tube cartridges as well as in quart, gallon and 5-gallon cans. While the cans are more economical, they're considerably messier for most jobs. Building paper (15# and 30#) and galvanized roofing nails (with and without rubber gaskets) conclude the list of materials you'll need for many roof repairs.

Aluminum roofing nails (for use with aluminum flashing)

Roof repair tools

Specialty tools you're likely to need when repairing roof systems include: Roof brackets and a sturdy plank (See page 86); a sharp utility knife with a roofer's blade; aviator snips or tin snips for cutting flashing; a roofing hammer (the hatchet-type end of the head is used for splitting wood shingles); and a hand seamer for bending small pieces of flashing.

How to install roof brackets

1 With the top of your extension ladder extending at least 3 ft. past the edge of the roof, lift a shingle tab on the farthest row of shingles you can reach comfortably (not higher than the fourth row). Attach the roof bracket to the roof sheathing by driving 16d. common nails through the slots on the top bracket flange, at rafter or truss locations.

2 Install another roof bracket no more than 4 ft. from the first. Use the lap lines on the shingles as a guide to make sure the brackets are level with one another. Insert a 2 × 8 or 2 × 10 plank (depending on the capacity of your roof brackets) into the brackets—there should be no more than 18 in. of overhang at each end. Install additional brackets if necessary. Anchor the plank by driving a roofing nail through the guide hole in the end of each bracket flange. After removing the brackets, cover the nail holes with roof cement (inset photo).

Fall-arresting gear

Personal fall-arrest systems (PFAS) are a smart investment if you'll be working on a sloped roof and need to remain mobile. A basic PFAS kit consists of a webbed body harness, shock-absorbing lanyard, locking rope grab, heavy-duty nylon lifeline and metal roof anchors. In the event you should fall, the body harness is designed to spread the impact of your weight over your shoulders, back and thighs to help reduce injury. The harness connects to a lifeline on the roof by way of a shock-absorbing lanyard with a snap ring on one end and a locking rope grab on the other. As you need to move up or down on the roof, the rope grab has a self-locking mechanism that allows you slide it up or down the lifeline by hand, but it locks in place as soon as you let go. In this way, the distance you fall is limited to the length of the lanyard. The heavy nylon lifeline snaps to a permanent or temporary metal roof anchor (see photo) that fastens to the roof decking with screws or nails. For safety's sake, be sure to exactly follow the manufacturer's instructions for installing and using the PFAS system you buy.

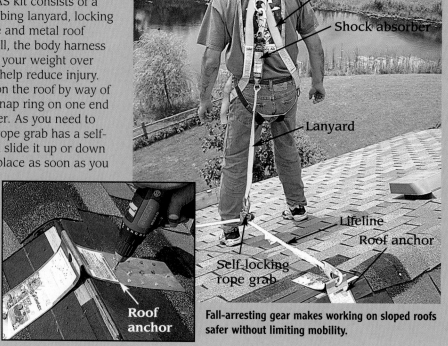

Fall-arresting gear makes working on sloped roofs safer without limiting mobility.

Repairing roof coverings

The roof covering is the first line of defense in protecting your home from the elements. While an estimated 80% or more of the roof coverings in America today are asphalt or fiberglass shingles, other low-maintenance roof covering products, such as concrete tiles, are growing quickly in popularity. But whether your roof is covered with asphalt shingles, cedar shakes, clay tiles or any of a number of less common coverings, maintaining and repairing the materials is of great importance to the health of your entire roof system.

Roof coverings develop problems for three or four primary reasons. The most frequent cause is simple wear and tear that is part of the natural aging process. Storms (especially those with strong wind and hail) likely account for the next highest number of problems. Inadequate ventilation and failure of other system parts, such as flashing, account for some types of damage, and improper installation of the roof coverings also can lead to premature roof failure.

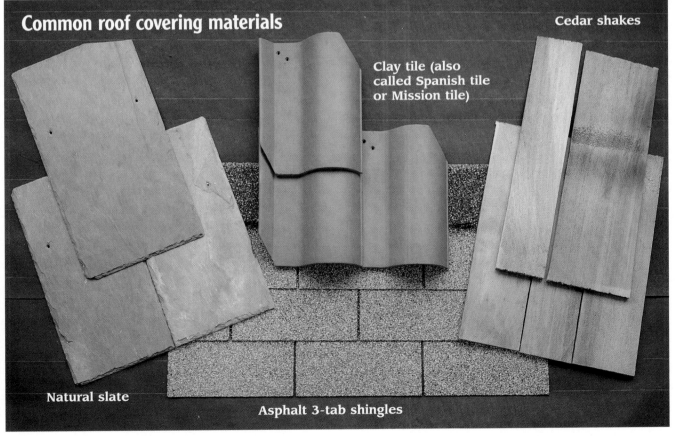

Common roof covering materials

Cedar shakes

Clay tile (also called Spanish tile or Mission tile)

Natural slate

Asphalt 3-tab shingles

Anatomy of an asphalt/fiberglass shingle roof

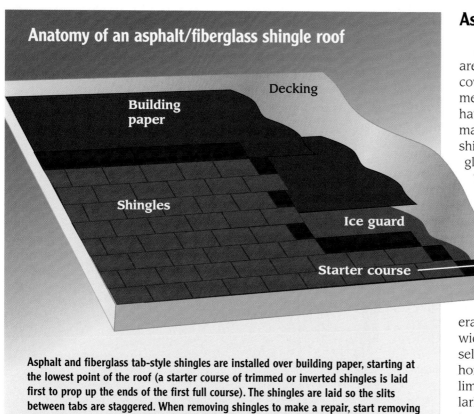

Asphalt and fiberglass tab-style shingles are installed over building paper, starting at the lowest point of the roof (a starter course of trimmed or inverted shingles is laid first to prop up the ends of the first full course). The shingles are laid so the slits between tabs are staggered. When removing shingles to make a repair, start removing at the highest row and work your way down.

Asphalt & fiberglass shingles

Asphalt and fiberglass shingles are by far the most popular roof covering material. While replacement is relatively easy, you may have a problem finding an exact match for older roofs. Most asphalt shingles sold today are "3-tab" shingles, measuring about 12 × 36 in. The bottom half is slotted to create three 12 in. tabs. An adhesive strip on the backside helps to secure the shingle to the building paper layer between the shingles and the roof decking. The mineral granule coatings come in a wide variety of colors, although selections at lumberyards and home improvement centers will be limited and tend to change regularly in accordance with design trends. You'll have better luck with a local roofing supply house. Remove a full shingle to use as a sample when looking for replacements. Match the color and weight (thickness) as closely as possible.

Choose a moderately warm day (60 to 75°F) to repair or replace asphalt shingles. If it's too cold, the shingles will be brittle and subject to further damage; if it's too hot, the replacements will be too soft to work with and the original shingles will be vulnerable to scuffing and other forms of damage (also, you

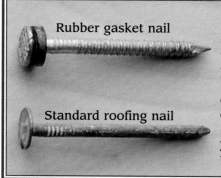

Roofing nails

Although most re-roof projects today are accomplished with pneumatic nailers and staplers (and appropriate coils of fasteners), roof repairs easily can be done with galvanized roofing nails (use 1½ in. nails for most jobs). If you can find rubber gasket nails, use them to attach flashing.

Rubber gasket nail

Standard roofing nail

Working with asphalt shingles

✔ Most shingle repair instructions you'll encounter (including those in this book) suggest that you begin the job by removing shingles above the repair area, then reinstall them when the fix is completed. But anyone who's actually tried this knows that removing asphalt shingles intact is next to impossible because the adhesive bands on the shingles bond them together. The chances of getting the shingles off whole are slightly better on colder days, although the asphalt shingles are almost as likely to break when cold as they are to rip when warm. Carefully slipping a thin prybar under the shingle and breaking the bond from the adhesive strip can meet with some success on occasion. But the bot-

tom line is don't get too discouraged if you get up on the roof and the first step of your repair procedure ends up by shredding a few shingles to get them out of the way. Either replace these shingles when the time comes to reinstall, or patch them back together as best you can with roof cement (be sure to drive nails near all edges).

✔ The asphalt foundation of asphalt shingles, coupled with the omnipresent roof cement, can cause some real messes as you try to do repair work. Tools gum up, flashings stick together—the stuff seems to get everywhere. The best solvent for cleaning asphalt is mineral spirits. Pour some into an old mosquito repellent bottle and carry it with you (along with a rag) as you work.

shouldn't be up on a roof on a hot day anyway).

Generally, it's easier (and equally effective) to repair small holes, cracks, loose shingles and other minor shingle damage with roof cement than it is to replace the entire shingle. For larger holes or damaged corners that have resulted in leaks, you can make a quick, temporary repair by slipping a flat piece of galvanized or aluminum flashing under the shingle until you can locate a replacement shingle. Cut the flashing to extend 4 in. beyond the sides of the hole and 2 in. above it. Remove any interfering nails. Apply roof cement to the underside of the flashing and slip it in place. Add more roof cement to create a seal over the top edge.

Emergency measures

If you're able to locate an active leak during or shortly after a rain storm, drive a 16d nail up through the leaking area of the sheathing, leaving part of the head exposed. Attach a string to the head of the nail to guide the water into a bucket. If the water is flowing down the underside of a rafter, tack a short block near the origin of the leak to stop the flow, then use a nail and string to divert the flow into the bucket.

If you can't fix the leak immediately (especially if it is large), and expect more rain, cover the roof over the leaking area with a plastic tarp or 6-mil polyethylene sheeting (you'll need at least one helper to do this). Extend the sheeting up over the ridge and anchor it with 1 × 4s tacked to the roof surface with 6d nails (after you remove the 1 × 4s, patch the nail holes with silicone caulk or roof cement.

CAUTION: Don't attempt to walk on the roof while it's wet.

Quick fixes for common problems

Cracked shingles. To repair a crack, lift up the shingle slightly and spread roof cement underneath both sides of the crack. Nail both sides down about 1 in. above the bottom edge. Apply additional roof cement to the crack and exposed nailheads.

Buckled shingles. To secure a loose or buckled shingle, first clean out any leaves or other debris underneath. If you encounter loose or popped nails, remove these and drive new nails next to them. Apply a liberal coat of roof cement under the shingle and press it firmly down into place.

How to repair damage from a popped nail

1 If a nail pops up through a shingle, remove the nail with a pry bar, being careful not to cause additional damage to the shingle.

2 If possible, carefully lift the overlapping shingle tab to expose the upper area of the lower shingle, where the popped nail was driven. Drive a new nail as close as possible to the one that was removed, and fill the old nail hole with roof cement. If you cannot get access to the lower shingle, drive a nail through the overlapping shingle near the old nail hole, then cover the nailhead with roof cement. It's important that you replace the removed nail.

3 Patch over the damage on the overlapping shingle by applying roof cement. If the bead is too thick, feather it back with a putty knife dipped in mineral spirits.

How to repair ridge cap shingles

Ridge cap shingles take a worse beating than field shingles. If only a few ridge shingles are damaged, you can replace just these; if ⅓ or more of the shingles show damage or wear, it's best to replace the entire ridge at once, so you don't have to keep going up every few years to make additional repairs. Typically, asphalt ridge shingles are installed starting at each gable end, working toward the center. You can either buy the ridge shingles separately, or cut them from 3-tab shingles. A closure shingle caps the joint where shingles meet.

1 If replacing all ridge cap shingles, start at the center, or closure shingle, and remove the ridge shingles in each direction until you reach the gable ends. Pull out all nails as you go. If you're only replacing a few individual shingles, remove only the ones you plan to replace. Work carefully to avoid damaging the shingles beneath the ridge cap.

2 After removing all the shingles, patch all nail holes and any cracks or other damage with roof cement. From each new 3-tab shingle, cut three 12-in. square ridge shingles, using the tab slots as guides. Cut the top corners at a 30° angle to prevent unsightly overlaps when the shingles are installed.

3 If needed, snap a chalkline 6 in. down from the peak on one side to align the replacement shingles. Install the first ridge shingle at one end, aligning it with the other ridge cap shingles. Drive roofing nails about ½ in. in from the angled edge, below the seal strip.

4 Continue installing ridge shingles from one end, leaving a 5-in. exposure (reveal) on each shingle until you reach the end of the repair area. Cut off any excess material where the shingles meet, then cut and install a closure shingle to cover the last seam. Cover exposed nailheads with roofing cement or clear silicone caulk.

How to replace damaged asphalt/fiberglass shingles

1 To replace a damaged shingle, carefully lift up the tabs of the shingles above it and loosen or pull out the nails with a flat pry bar. Three-tab shingles typically have four nails holding them. If shingles are closely spaced, you may also need to remove nails from the next course above. If you're removing more than one shingle in the repair area, start with the highest shingle and work down to the lowest. Be careful not to damage surrounding shingles. NOTE: if the shingles are too brittle to work with, soften them with a hair dryer or a heat gun on low setting.

2 Remove the rest of the shingles, up to and including the damaged shingles. Repair any holes or tears in the building paper layer with roof cement.

3 Begin installing the replacement shingle or shingles, starting with the lowest course. If the shingles have adhesive strips (seal lines) on the back, remove the clear protective tape backing before installing the shingle. Do not use the same nail holes and make sure the nails will be hidden by the shingle above. Typically, a roofing nail is driven about 1 in. above each tab slot and near each end of the shingle.

4 Slip the shingles in the highest replacement course beneath the tabs of the course just above the repair area. You may need to trim the tops of the new shingles slightly if they're obstructed by nails. Don't trim off so much material that the new shingle is not well covered at the top edge by the tabs from the row above. Lift the tabs above and nail the last row of shingles in position.

TIP: If you have trouble lifting the tabs in the shingle course above the repair area high enough to allow for hammering, lift them just high enough to push the nail points into the replacement shingle. Then, place one end of your pry bar on the nailhead, and the other on a wood block. Rap the pry bar with a hammer to drive the nail home.

5 Replace any roofing nails that you removed in the shingle courses above the repair area that were left intact. Don't use the same nail holes. Patch any nail holes or minor damage with roof cement.

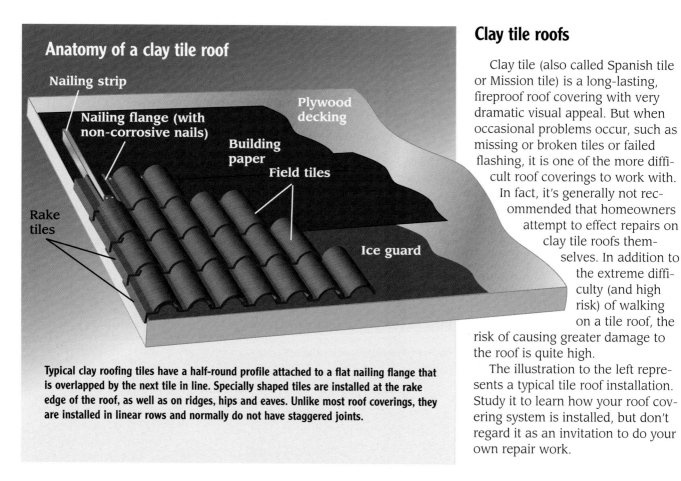

Anatomy of a clay tile roof

Nailing strip

Nailing flange (with non-corrosive nails)

Plywood decking

Building paper

Field tiles

Rake tiles

Ice guard

Typical clay roofing tiles have a half-round profile attached to a flat nailing flange that is overlapped by the next tile in line. Specially shaped tiles are installed at the rake edge of the roof, as well as on ridges, hips and eaves. Unlike most roof coverings, they are installed in linear rows and normally do not have staggered joints.

Clay tile roofs

Clay tile (also called Spanish tile or Mission tile) is a long-lasting, fireproof roof covering with very dramatic visual appeal. But when occasional problems occur, such as missing or broken tiles or failed flashing, it is one of the more difficult roof coverings to work with.

In fact, it's generally not recommended that homeowners attempt to effect repairs on clay tile roofs themselves. In addition to the extreme difficulty (and high risk) of walking on a tile roof, the risk of causing greater damage to the roof is quite high.

The illustration to the left represents a typical tile roof installation. Study it to learn how your roof covering system is installed, but don't regard it as an invitation to do your own repair work.

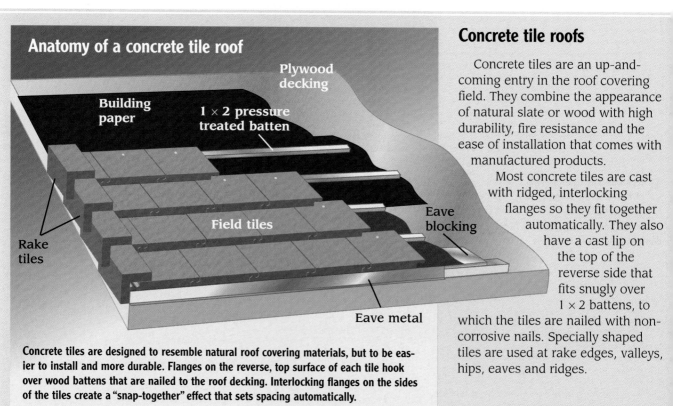

Anatomy of a concrete tile roof

Plywood decking

Building paper

1 × 2 pressure treated batten

Field tiles

Eave blocking

Rake tiles

Eave metal

Concrete tiles are designed to resemble natural roof covering materials, but to be easier to install and more durable. Flanges on the reverse, top surface of each tile hook over wood battens that are nailed to the roof decking. Interlocking flanges on the sides of the tiles create a "snap-together" effect that sets spacing automatically.

Concrete tile roofs

Concrete tiles are an up-and-coming entry in the roof covering field. They combine the appearance of natural slate or wood with high durability, fire resistance and the ease of installation that comes with manufactured products.

Most concrete tiles are cast with ridged, interlocking flanges so they fit together automatically. They also have a cast lip on the top of the reverse side that fits snugly over 1 × 2 battens, to which the tiles are nailed with non-corrosive nails. Specially shaped tiles are used at rake edges, valleys, hips, eaves and ridges.

Slate shingle roofs

Replacing slate shingles requires caution: slate roofs are slippery, and the shingles may crack if you walk on them. If you need to get on the roof, hook a ladder over the ridge or construct a chicken ladder to help distribute your weight.

If you need to cut slate shingles to size, rent a wet saw or bring the shingles to a tile/slate dealer to have the cuts made for you. The installation methods for slate tiles are similar to those for wood shake roofs (See page 96). The main difference is that the tiles are heavy and usually need to be supported by a temporary nailer as they're attached by driving non-corrosive nails through pre-drilled guide holes in the tiles.

Anatomy of a slate shingle roof

Plywood decking

Non-corrosive nails

Building paper

Field tiles

Ice guard

Starter course

Slate shingle roofs are among the most coveted roof types because their natural beauty and pleasing irregularity create a distinctive Old-world feeling. They're installed in much the same fashion as wood shake roofs.

Concrete tile roofs are only installed by contractors who work directly with the tile manufacturers or distributors. Consequently, they're usually covered by long-term warranties so you should not ever need to make repairs yourself except in dire emergencies. In fact, trying to repair the roof yourself may violate the terms of your warranty.

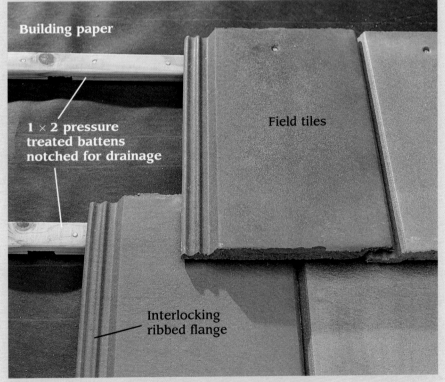

Building paper

1 × 2 pressure treated battens notched for drainage

Field tiles

Interlocking ribbed flange

Concrete roofing tiles have the appearance of slate and other natural roof covering materials, but are easier to install and usually less expensive.

Anatomy of a wood shake roof

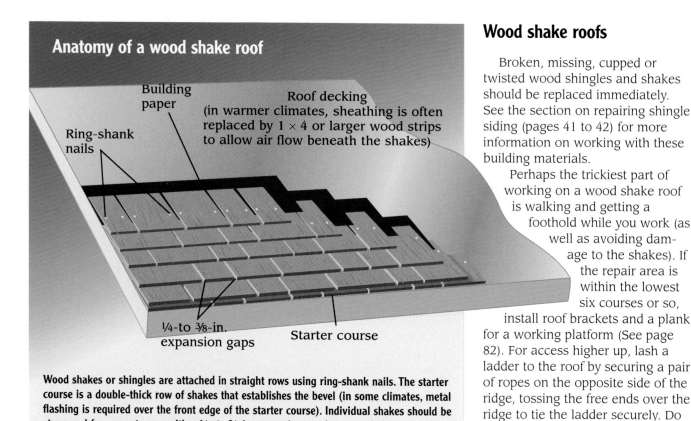

Wood shakes or shingles are attached in straight rows using ring-shank nails. The starter course is a double-thick row of shakes that establishes the bevel (in some climates, metal flashing is required over the front edge of the starter course). Individual shakes should be staggered from row to row with a ¼- to ⅜-in. expansion gap between shakes.

Wood shake roofs

Broken, missing, cupped or twisted wood shingles and shakes should be replaced immediately. See the section on repairing shingle siding (pages 41 to 42) for more information on working with these building materials.

Perhaps the trickiest part of working on a wood shake roof is walking and getting a foothold while you work (as well as avoiding damage to the shakes). If the repair area is within the lowest six courses or so, install roof brackets and a plank for a working platform (See page 82). For access higher up, lash a ladder to the roof by securing a pair of ropes on the opposite side of the ridge, tossing the free ends over the ridge to tie the ladder securely. Do not attempt this alone.

How to replace a wood roof shake or shingle

1 Split the damaged shake or shingle with a wood chisel and remove the pieces.

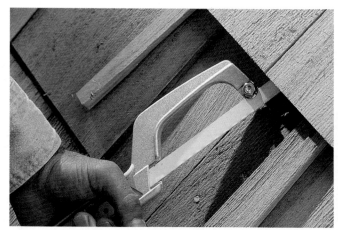

2 Drive wood shims under the shingles in the course above to create access, then cut off nailheads with a hacksaw blade.

3 Cut a replacement shake to fit and slip it into place, aligning the butt ends to the ones on each side. Then, pull the shake back out about 1 in. Drive two nails through the shake at an angle, just below the upper row of shakes.

4 Dab a bit of clear silicone caulk on the nail-heads, then use a hammer and wood block to drive the shake up into place.

Built-up roofs

Most older flat roofs (or nearly flat roofs) are made of alternating layers of building felt and hot-mopped asphalt or coal tar, topped with gravel or crushed rock. Called "Built-up roofs" or a variety of other names, such as "tar-and-gravel", they are relatively "low-tech" roofs that are usually reliable and are easy to maintain. The principal tool you'll need to maintain a built-up roof is a big bucket of roof cement (many building centers sell roof cement in economical 5-gallon pails).

Common problems that occur on built-up roofs include cracking and blistering of the built-up surface. The essential formula for dealing with these problems is to clean them up as best you can, then smear them with roof cement. Repairing larger problem areas is somewhat more involved (as noted in the tip box below). For big holes and cracks, you need to actually remove sections of the roof, then rebuild them using roof cement and building paper in much the same way the roof was built up originally.

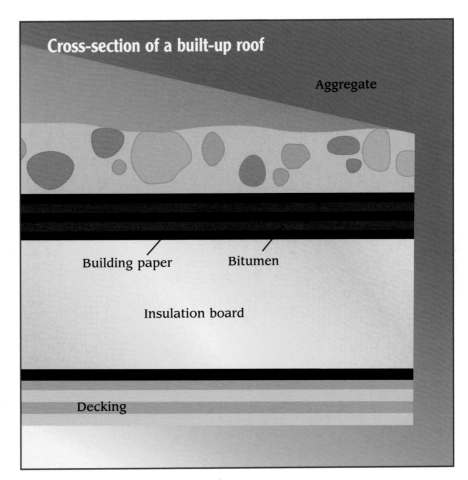

Cross-section of a built-up roof

Aggregate

Building paper   Bitumen

Insulation board

Decking

Patching cracks & blisters in built-up roofs

Small cracks. If the roof is topped with gravel or crushed rock, sweep it away from the repair area with a whisk broom or stiff brush. Clean out any small cracks or holes and fill with roof cement. Apply a liberal coat, feathering out the edges at least 3 in. on either side.

Small blisters. Slice open smaller blisters with a utility knife. If only the top layer or two are blistered, cut only down to the point where the paper has separated from the layers beneath, leaving the lower layers intact. If the layers beneath are damp, allow them to dry (you can speed up the drying process by using a hair dryer or a heat gun set on "low" temperature). Use a putty knife to apply roof cement under each side of the cut, then fasten the edges down with roofing nails spaced about 3 in apart. Apply a second, liberal coat of roof cement over the crack and nailheads, feathering out 3 in. on all sides. TIP: Frequently dip the utility knife and putty knife in a can of mineral spirits to prevent a buildup of cement or tar on the blade. Cut a patch of 15-lb. building felt that overlaps the repair area by 3 in. on all sides. Embed the patch into the roof cement and nail in place, spacing nails a few inches apart. Cover the patch with a second coat of roof cement, then replace the gravel by pressing it into the wet cement.

Larger cracks & blisters. To repair large blisters, cracks or buckled sections, you'll need to cut out the old roofing down to the sheathing, then rebuild the cutout area with one or more patches. Remove any gravel from the damaged area and several inches outside it. With a utility knife, cut out a square or rectangle that includes the damaged portion, down to the sheathing. Pay special attention to possible sources of the leak outside the damaged area, such as a nearby hole, crack or leaky vent flashing. Scrape off any old cement with a wide putty knife. Using one of the old damaged layers as a template, cut one or more replacement patches to fit snugly into the cutout area. For built-up roofs, you'll need several layers of 15-lb. felt, sandwiched between coats of cement to make the patch flush with the surrounding roofing. Start by covering the sheathing with a thick, even layer of roofing cement, working under the edges of the cutout area. Press the first patch into the cement, spread a coat of cement over the top, embed the second patch, and continue until you've built up the patch flush to the surrounding roofing. Coat the patched area and several inches beyond each side with roof cement. Cut an oversized patch that overlaps each edge by 2 in. Embed the patch in the cement and nail it down with 1½-in. roofing nails. Apply a final coat of cement over the patch (cover the edges and nailheads) and replace the gravel.

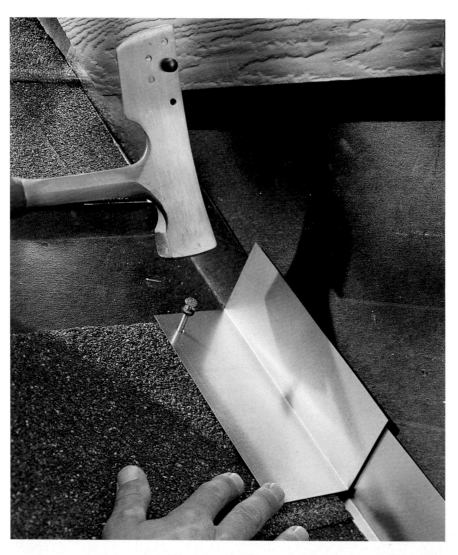

Flashings are used to seal gaps around projections through a roof (vents, chimneys, dormers), as well as at roof valleys, eaves and gable ends. Because these areas are the primary stress points on a roof, they are often the first to develop problems and are common spots for leaks to occur.

Most flashing materials are metal, usually thin-gauge galvanized steel or aluminum. Some aluminum flashing has a baked-on enamel finish (for some reason, white and brown seem to be the only color options). Flashing is sold in rolls, which you can bend to fit a desired profile, or preformed shapes such as valley flashing, step flashing, vent flashing and drip edges.

Aluminum and galvanized metal flashings generally will outlast one or maybe even two wood or asphalt roofs. However, once the flashings begin to show signs of wear, rust or corrosion, plan on replacing all the flashings the next time you reroof your house. But if the flashings

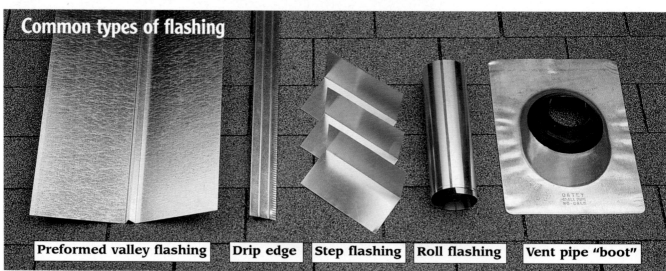

Common types of flashing

Preformed valley flashing   **Drip edge**   **Step flashing**   **Roll flashing**   **Vent pipe "boot"**

Flashing can be purchased preformed or you can buy light-gauge metal, then cut and shape it to fit your project. Most types of preformed flashing can be purchased in galvanized steel or in aluminum. *Preformed valley flashing* is approximately 2 ft. wide and usually has an inverted "V" that runs lengthwise down the center of each 10 ft. strip to help maintain rigidity and prevent water from puddling. Metal drip edge is fastened to the eaves and rakes of a roof to prevent water

runoff from trickling down the fascia. Step flashing is interwoven with shingles to seal around dormers, chimneys and skylights. Roll flashing can be bent to make valley flashing, step flashing, upper and lower saddles, and just about any specialty flashing you can imagine. Vent pipe "boots" consist of a metal base attached to a neoprene rubber sleeve that fits over and seals DWV (drain/waste/vent) or natural gas exhaust pipes.

show signs of failure, don't wait for the shingles to catch up to them. Make repairs right away.

Although the job flashing performs is relatively simple, and working successfully with flashing is mostly a matter of paying attention, many handymen are a little intimidated by the prospect of repairing or installing flashing. In fact, some types of flashing, such as vent pipe boots and drip edge, are easier to install than shingles. Others, such as step flashing and chimney counterflashing, are slightly more complex. The trick is to study the way the flashing fits together carefully. Once you understand the "theory," you'll be amazed how easy it is to put it into practice.

As with most types of exterior repairs, you have two basic options with flashings: Repair them or replace them. Because replacing usually involves stripping off some of the roof covering, the preferred option is usually to repair. Repairs can be as simple as applying gutter lap caulk over deterioration or damage, or refreshing the roof cement seal surrounding the flashing pieces.

When repairing or replacing flashings, always use patches and replacement pieces made of the same material—using dissimilar metals causes an electrolytic reaction that results in corrosion. Use galvanized nails with galvanized flashings, and aluminum nails with aluminum flashings.

The theory of flashing

Understanding the basic concept of how it works will take you a long way toward becoming comfortable working with flashing. Flashing is all about making transitions between two different types of building materials. To perform this job effectively, it must have the ability to move without leaving the transition area exposed. When temperatures and humidity levels change, building materials expand and contract at different rates. Because of this fact of nature, roof decking that butted up flush to a chimney chase one day can shift away the next, creating a gap that could allow moisture and pests into your home. But even though metal also expands and contracts at its own pace, a good flashing system will continue to cover the transition area whether there is a gap or not. In this example, the flashing works because it is a two-part system. Metal counter flashing embedded in the mortar joints of the chimney is folded down over the top of metal step flashing that is woven into and over the shingles. The two parts are not connected, except by a layer of elastic roof cement, and therefore they can move independently. As you work to make repairs on flashing, keep this basic relationship in mind: Each piece of flashing can only be permanently fastened to one of the materials it transitions between.

How to repair pinholes in flashing

1 Pinholes in metal flashing are caused by corrosion or rusting that weakens the metal and, little by little, begin to allow water to seep through. While not overly serious, they do indicate that the flashing is perhaps past its prime and will require full replacement before long. In the meantime, the immediate problem can be addressed easily with gutter lap or butyl rubber caulk (visually, gutter lap will blend in with the metal better). First, scrub the affected area with medium to fine steel wool, then wipe it clean with mineral spirits. Apply gutter lap over the area with a caulk gun (on broad surfaces, apply the gutter lap in a wavy pattern that can be feathered out).

2 With a putty knife dipped in mineral spirits, smooth out the gutter lap and feather it slightly to remove ridges where the material meets the flashing. Inspect the area once or twice a year to look for further damage and refresh the gutter lap as needed.

How to repair rusty flashing

1 Clean off as much of the rust as you can, using fine sandpaper (180- to 220-grit) and a wire brush. The more rust you remove, the longer it will take to reestablish itself.

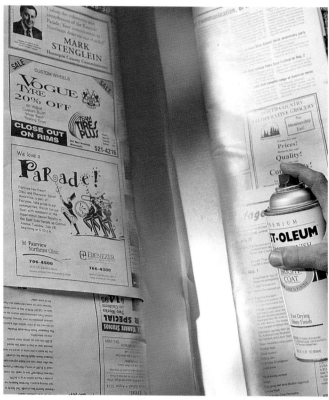

2 Wipe the flashing clean with mineral spirits, then mask off the adjoining shingles with tape and newspaper. Spray the rusted area with exterior rated aluminum spray paint to seal out moisture and renew the appearance. If working on a small run of flashing, paint the entire run for a more uniform appearance.

Metal roll flashing (galvanized steel or aluminum) can be hand-bent to fit your repair project needs using a flat bending surface with a straightedge.

Bending your own flashing

Fabricating roll flashing into usable sizes and shapes is an easy alternative to spending a lot of money on preformed flashings or having flashing custom bent at a metal shop. While there are many "tricks of the trade" offering clever ways to make your own flashing, the simplest solutions are often the best you'll encounter. All you really need to set up an on-site flashing fabrication center is a sawhorse with a straightedge attached parallel to one side of the sawhorse top. Simply attach the straightedge so the distance to the parallel edge of the sawhorse equals the planned width of the flashing. Then, cut a piece of roll flashing to length with aviator snips and lay it on top of the sawhorse so a factory edge is flush against the straightedge. Wearing gloves, crease the roll flashing so it follows the edge of the sawhorse top and forms a 90° bend (crease a little at a time and work your way from one end to the other to avoid kinking).

Parts of a chimney & chimney flashing system

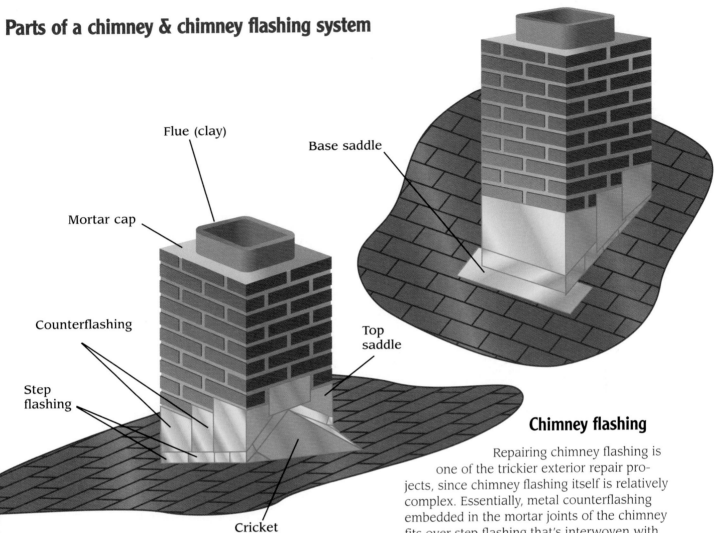

Flue (clay)

Base saddle

Mortar cap

Counterflashing

Top saddle

Step flashing

Cricket

Chimney flashing

Repairing chimney flashing is one of the trickier exterior repair projects, since chimney flashing itself is relatively complex. Essentially, metal counterflashing embedded in the mortar joints of the chimney fits over step flashing that's interwoven with the shingles. An upper saddle bent to follow the top corners covers the top pieces of step and counterflashing, and the lower step and counterflashing pieces overlap a simple saddle at the low end of the chimney. The ends of the base saddle are bent up and around the bottom corner of the chimney (but are overlapped by the step and counterflashing. A cricket (See next page) can be added to encourage water runoff.

While the above situation is the preferred way to flash a chimney, many chimney flashings consist of step and base flashings only, with the top edges embedded into the mortar joints, or simply adhered to the side of the chimney with roof cement in lieu of counterflashing. On the uphill side, the top flashing may not extend far enough up under the shingles to protect the roof deck against the accumulation of water behind the chimney. If the chimney was improperly flashed in the first place, you'll need to remove all the old flashing and reflash the chimney correctly.

Repairing a mortar cap

While loose or damaged flashing causes a great many chimney leaks, water can also enter through a damaged or improperly sealed mortar cap. These leaks are harder to detect because the water runs down between the masonry facing and the flue tiles. The leak usually shows up as a wet spot on the ceiling or wall above the fireplace, or as a drip at the front edge of the fireplace opening.

On most older homes, the caps were made of the same type of mortar used to lay up the brick chimney; on newer homes, chimneys have longer-lasting reinforced concrete caps, which overhang the top of the chimney by a few inches to prevent water from running down the brickwork. If you have a badly damaged mortared or concrete cap, consider having it replaced with a new concrete one. Because the new cap often requires complicated formwork and reinforcement, it's a job best left to a masonry contractor.

If the chimney cap is sound but has developed small cracks, fill these with liquid concrete crack filler or concrete repair caulk (See pages 18 to 19). There should be expansion joints left between the inside edges of the cap and flue. Instead of concrete caulk, seal this joint with silicone caulk.

Sealing chimney flashings

If the chimney flashings are in good condition but cracks and gaps have developed around them, reseal all gaps and joints between the flashing pieces and the roof and chimney. Scrape out the old roof cement with a stiff putty knife (this may take some effort), and replace with polyurethane caulk. Use the same techniques to reattach loose flashings. To reseal the tops of counterflashings where they fit into the mortar joints, remove any loose or crumbling mortar to a depth of about 1/2 in. and replace with caulk.

Chimney flashings usually show the worst deterioration at or near the areas where they meet the roof. You can patch holes, cracks and tears in flashing by coating the affected areas with a thick layer of fibered plastic roof cement. However, consider this a temporary fix only: Plastic and asphalt-type roof cements last only a few years, at best.

How to replace counterflashing

1 Cut any roof cement seals and carefully pry the damaged pieces of counterflashing out of the mortar joints using sturdy pliers. You may need to chip out some of the mortar to free the piece. If the mortar is loose or crumbling, remove all the pieces in the affected area.

A cricket is created by custom-fabricated medium-gauge sheet metal to fit over a plywood half-pyramid that's butted up against the top edge of a chimney. The flanges (tabs) on the metal cricket covering should lay flat on the roof and against the back of the chimney. The cricket is installed over the building paper layer—attach the flanges to the roof deck with roof cement and rubber-gasket roofing nails, and attach the vertical flanges to the chimney with roof cement only. Trim the top saddle to straddle the top of the cricket. You'll need to add a piece of counterflashing (in most cases) to fit over the peak area of the cricket.

Installing a chimney cricket

A cricket is installed along the top edge of a chimney to divert water runoff, prevent debris from accumulating and prevent erosion of the flashing caused by torrents of water runoff during heavy rains. Crickets are especially useful on steep-sloped roofs (greater than a 4-in-12 pitch). The main reason more people don't have crickets installed along the tops of their chimneys is that you can't purchase them in stores. Because chimney width and roof pitch varies so much, its left to the homeowners or roofing contractors to fabricate and install a custom cricket.

By taking careful measurements of the size and pitch of the roof area above your chimney, you should be able to lay out and fashion your own cricket (See photo and caption, left). Use 1/2-in. or 3/4-in. exterior plywood for the base structure and medium-gauge galvanized sheet metal (about 28 gauge) to make the metal cricket top.

On shallow roofs, you can shingle over the cricket (attach the shingle with roof cement, not nails), but more frequently the shingles are trimmed away at the edges of the cricket.

2 Cut and bend replacement pieces from the same type of metal. Using a cold chisel and hammer, remove 1 in. of mortar from the joint (or enough so the bent portion of the flashing can be inserted completely into the joint). Instead of a cold chisel and hammer, an angle grinder with a masonry cutoff disc can be used to remove the mortar, as shown above.

3 Use a hand seamer or locking pliers with a seaming jaw to bend counterflashing so it fits around the corners of the chimney. You'll need to make a relief cut in the top corner of each piece. Apply roof cement to the backsides of the replacement flashing pieces and press them into place so the flanges are fully seated in the mortar joint areas.

4 Dampen the joint above the flashing, then pack new mortar into it with a pointing trowel or joint filler tool. Allow the mortar to set up (firm, but not hard) and tool it with a grooving tool to match surrounding joints.

5 After the mortar has dried completely (let it dry for a minimum of 3 to 4 days), seal the areas where the new counterflashing overlaps the step flashing using roof cement or polyurethane caulk.

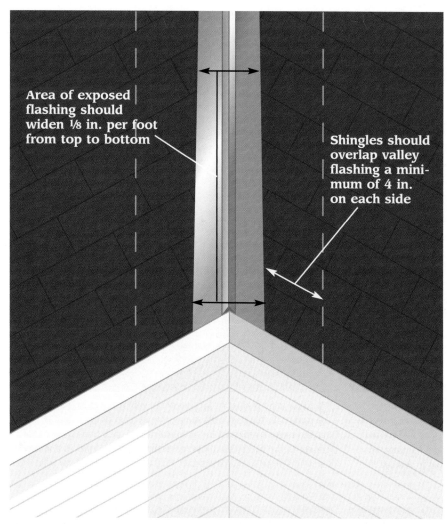

Area of exposed flashing should widen ⅛ in. per foot from top to bottom

Shingles should overlap valley flashing a minimum of 4 in. on each side

Metal valley flashing provides a durable channel where roof sections intersect, resisting damage while directing water runoff off the roof.

Roof valleys must be flashed due to the large amount of water that they collect from adjoining roof surfaces and direct off the roof. Leaks often occur near the bottom end due to the force of water gushing down the valley, which can work its way underneath the surrounding shingles. Because they carry so much water and the broad metal surfaces have a high degree of exposure, valley flashings are more prone to damage than many other flashing types.

Valley flashings can be formed from a variety of materials, although most preformed valley flashing is made of galvanized metal or aluminum (See page 98). Preformed valley flashings typically have an inverted "V" spine running lengthwise to increase rigidity and and prevent puddling and debris accumulation. This type of open valley flashing is sold in 10-ft.-long strips. For new installations or repairing large sections of non-preformed valley flashing, you can purchase wide metal roll flashing. Roll flashing can be used for seamless runs of up to 50 ft., but it is slightly more prone to buckling than lapped valley flashing. For best results, precrease the flashing on the ground before installing it on the roof, aligning the crease over the centerline of the valley area.

Tips for repairing valley flashing

✔ If you notice leaks, open joints or damaged shingles at the lower end of the valley only, the shingles may be too close together. Typically, the distance between shingles across the valley should be farther apart at the bottom than at the top: The space should widen ⅛ in. per foot from the ridge to the eaves. For example, on a 12-ft. valley, if the distance across the exposed portion of flashing is 5 in. at the top end, it should be 6½ in. at the bottom end. If the valley channel is too narrow, determine the proper width at the low end (relative to the top end), snap two chalklines and trim back the shingles with aviator snips. Also, the top edge of each shingle should be "dubbed", or cut off at a 45° angle so the edges don't trap water running down the valley. NOTE: Do not trim back shingles so far that they overlap the valley by less than 6 in.

✔ If the flashing has surface rust or corrosion but is still sound, you can extend its life and enhance the appearance by coating it with a rust-preventative paint, which you can apply by brush or from spray cans. You can either use an aluminum-colored paint or a color that closely matches the house trim or siding. Sand off rust spots down to bare metal with 180-grit silicon carbide sandpaper, and wipe the area clean with a rag dampened in mineral spirits. Apply two coats of paint following label directions (See page 100).

Closed valley flashing

On closed valleys (often used on asphalt composition roofs) the metal flashing is hidden beneath a layer of interwoven or overlapping shingles, which must be removed to repair or replace the flashing. Some closed valleys may be flashed with heavy roll roofing instead of metal. Repair and maintain these valleys as you would treat the rest of the asphalt roof.

How valley flashing is installed:
Open valley flashing is installed after the building paper layer but before the shingles, beginning at the eave area of the roof. The overhang is trimmed to follow the lines of the drip edge. The flashing should overhang the drip edge slightly (not more than ⅛ in. or so). On runs longer than 10 ft., additional strips of valley flashing are lapped over the lower strip (about a 6-to 12-in. overlap). These laps should be sealed with roof cement. At the roof ridge, a notch is cut out at the spine so the top ends of the flashing strip can be folded back over the ridge and fastened to the roof deck (if the valley meets a side wall, the ends are folded up under the siding or wall counterflashing).

In some areas of severe weather, codes require that the outer edges of metal valley flashing be folded over in a 1-in. hem. This creates a dam that helps prevent water or ice from getting beneath the shingles.

TIP: Refresh the seal between valley flashing and the adjoining trimmed shingles by removing deteriorated roof cement and applying new roof cement with a caulk gun. This will prevent water from coursing out of the valley and beneath the shingle layer.

How to patch leaks in open valley flashing

1 To patch larger holes, cracks or rusted-through areas, first measure the damaged area and cut a patch of slightly larger dimensions from the same style valley flashing material. The patch should be wide enough to slip 2 in. underneath the shingles on both sides, and extend at least 2 in. above and below the damage. Clean the area around the hole with a wire brush, then cut the seal between the flashing and adjoining shingles with a utility knife. Apply a layer of roof cement to the area with a wide putty knife, then press the patch in place.

2 Apply more cement around the edges of the patch and feather out with a putty knife dipped in mineral spirits.

Step flashing

Step flashing is a unique type of flashing because it is interwoven with the roof shingles to form a single, mixed media water barrier. It is much easier to install when done during a full reroof project, but it can be replaced without too much difficulty.

You can purchase step flashing in preformed ells of various size (8 in. long with 4 in. flanges is a common size). Or, you can bend your own from roll flashing.

Step flashing is installed wherever a roof meets a vertical wall or surface: chimneys, dormers and skylights being the most common applications. Skylight curbs frequently are flashed with flashing kits that are sold as accessories with the skylight unit. Normally, the step flashing (like the rest of the kit) is made of aluminum with a baked-on brown enamel finish. If you need to replace step flashing of this type, you don't have to purchase an entire new flashing kit. Simply buy some matching roll flashing, cut it to size with aviator snips and bend the step flashing pieces to fit.

Siding strips overlap tops of step flashing

Building paper should run 4 to 6 in. up vertical surface

Step flashing is interwoven in alternating layers with the shingles. The key to installing it is to make sure that the bottom edges of all step flashing pieces lap over the surface of shingle to direct water runoff over the shingles (not beneath them). The tops of the step flashing are covered by siding or counterflashing.

How to replace step flashing

1 If possible, remove the siding on wall abutting the repair area (See pages 34 to 49). Otherwise, pry the siding laps as far away from the wall as you can and prop them out to allow access to the step flashing pieces. If working in a chimney area, simply bend the counterflashing up and out of the way. With a utility knife, cut roof cement seals holding the flashing in place. Carefully pull back the shingles to expose the flashing and pry out the piece or pieces with a flat pry bar.

2 Cut pieces of galvanized or aluminum roll flashing (whichever metal type is used for the original flashing) to the same size as the original flashing pieces, then carefully crease the replacement pieces along the center by folding them over a straightedge. If the old step flashing was a standard size, you can purchase preformed step flashing ells instead of taking the time to bend your own.

3 If one of the pieces of step flashing you're replacing was at the bottom or top of the step flashing run, it probably was bent or cut to fit around the corner (or to allow the straight flashing at the top or bottom edge of the flashed object to fit over it). Use the original piece as a reference to cut a new piece with the same size and shape.

4 Coat the back of the lowest piece of flashing and the installation area with roof cement. Slip the flashing into position and secure it with one rubber-gasket roofing nail driven into the roof deck about 1 in. down from the top edge of the flashing. Do not nail the flashing to the vertical surface.

5 Attach another piece of step flashing over the first. The top edge of the new piece should be roughly even with the top edge of the adjacent shingle. Apply roof cement to the upper portion of the first flashing piece, and overlap it by at least 4 in. with the new piece. Nail the new piece near the top edge. Next, install a shingle in the lowest course where shingles were removed, following the pattern of the shingle installation. Bond the shingle to the flashing with roof cement.

6 Finish installing shingles and step flashing in the repair area, alternating between shingles and flashing to create the required interwoven effect. Don't skimp on the roof cement, and take care not to nail through a shingle and into a piece of flashing. Apply roof cement over any exposed nailheads, then bend down counterflashing or reattach siding. Apply roof cement in the gaps between flashing pieces (this includes the gaps between step and counterflashing).

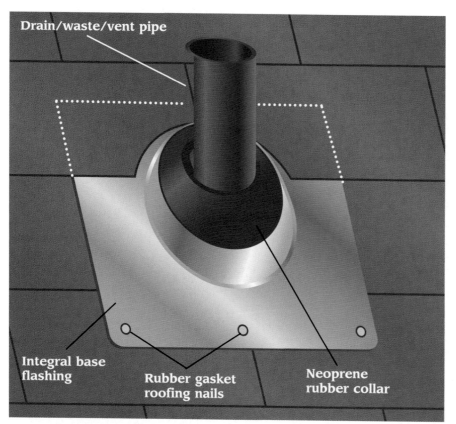

Drain/waste/vent pipe

Integral base flashing

Rubber gasket roofing nails

Neoprene rubber collar

Vent pipe flashing has improved dramatically over the years, and is now one of the easier flashing types to install. The neoprene rubber collar fits tightly over the vent pipe and, because it's factory sealed to the metal base flashing, it seldom fails.

Vent pipe flashing

Rather than trying to patch damaged or rusted flashings around vent pipes and similar projections through the roof, you'll likely find it easier and more effective to install new flashing. You can buy preformed flashing units with neoprene rubber seals to fit a variety of smaller pipe diameters (up to 4 in.), as well as all-metal flashings and storm collars for larger diameters. These handy flashing units are far easier to install and more effective than the old galvanized metal tube-and-collar assemblies like the one being removed in *Step 1* on the next page.

If the shingle or shingles you remove when replacing a vent boot are in good shape, re-use them. Otherwise, use them as templates for cutting new shingles to fit around the vent pipe.

Resealing a metal boot

Drain/waste/vent pipes are not the only pipes to vent through many roofs. If your home is heated with natural gas or has a natural gas fireplace, it's quite likely that you have a metal gas vent pipe protruding through your roof. Because the exhaust from the natural gas can be hot, it's not advised that you use neoprene rubber boots to flash gas vent pipes. Instead, use an all-metal boot that's sealed at the top with heat-resistant caulk.

The downside to this type of vent pipe flashing is that the top seal is prone to develop leaks as it undergoes constant temperature changes from the exhaust. This causes even top-quality heat-resistant caulk to break down eventually. If this happens, you can try to refresh the old caulk with new material as you would with any roof cement seal. But for added protection, wrap aluminum tape around the seal at the top of the flashing collar. In addition to forming an extra layer of protection against moisture, the tape also reflects sunlight, which accelerates the degradation of most caulking materials. Make sure the vent pipe and boot are clean and dry before you apply the aluminum tape.

How to replace vent pipe flashing

1 Remove the old flashing boot. Carefully remove the shingle or shingles directly above the flashing to expose the base. Cut the seal and remove any nails, then slip the old flashing off the pipe.

2 Clean any old cement off the pipe with a wire brush. Apply a bead of roof cement around the perimeter of the underside of the boot base. Slip the new flashing boot over the pipe, tucking the top edge underneath the shingles above. Fasten the top edges and center of the base with roofing nails (to be covered by the replacement shingles), and daub the nailheads with roof cement.

3 Push the neoprene rubber collar down flush to the flashing base. The rubber collar fits tightly over the pipe, so there's no need to caulk the joints. Drive rubber gasket nails near the corners of the base. Also drive one intermediate nail per side.

4 Reattach the shingle or install replacement shingles. Make sure the top of the flashing base is covered by shingle tabs. Dab roof cement over any nail holes or exposed nailheads.

Repairing gutters

Gutter systems catch water runoff and direct it away from the house. Unless repaired promptly, even small leaks or overflows can result in big problems, such as peeling paint, rotted siding and trim, leaks around windows and doors, sinking foundations, wet basements, soil erosion and beaten-down plants in flower beds. Common problems that plague gutters include rust, peeling paint, leaky joints, debris buildup, sags or improper slope and ice or snow damage. Inspect and clean your gutters and downspouts at least twice a year; once in early spring before heavy rains start, and once in the fall after tree leaves drop.

This section includes basic repairs you can make to keep gutters leak-free and flowing. But in some cases, repairs won't help and you'll need to replace the gutter system. Replacing a gutter system is a relatively easy do-it-yourself project, as there are a variety of "snap-together" systems on the market, in galvanized steel, aluminum and vinyl, that can be installed with only a few basic tools. In snap-together systems, the gutter sections (typically 10 ft. long) are connected with snap-in-place connectors or sleeves and have snap-on end caps. The main drawback is that they can develop leaks at connection points. Seamless gutters, another new gutter option, consist of continuous gutter lengths, joined only at inside and outside corners and at down-spout drop outlets. They're less prone to leaking but must be fabricated on site by a professional installer.

Gutter repair materials

Materials used to repair gutter systems include: (A) fiberglass repair fabric; (B) aluminum-faced repair tape; (C) pop rivets; (D) sheet metal screws; (E) roof cement; (F) clear gutter lap elasticized repair caulk (metal gutter system formulation); (G) colored gutter sealant for colored metal gutter systems; (H) all-purpose seam caulk for plastic or metal gutters.

Gutter slope

If you notice that a gutter overflows during a heavy rain storm, but is not otherwise clogged, or has standing water in it, the gutter doesn't have enough slope to flow properly. The cause could be a sag, due to loose hangers, a settling foundation, snow or ice damage, or a tree limb or ladder that whacked it out of alignment. Or, the gutter could have been installed improperly in the first place. No matter what the cause, you'll need to rehang the gutter.

First, check the slope. If the gutter is loose or sagging, you may be able to determine the original slope by inspecting the fascia board behind it. If the gutter was installed at the wrong slope, you'll need to remove it and rehang it. In both cases, check the slope with a 6-ft. level, (or a smaller level on top of a long straightedge) in several places. The gutter should slope toward the downspout at a rate of about ¼ in. per 4 ft. of run. Do not gauge the slope by the eave line, as the foundation may have settled unevenly.

To fix a sagging gutter, snap a chalkline that follows the correct slope. Loosen or remove the hangers within and near the sag. Have a helper lift up the gutter until it is flush with the chalkline, then reattach or replace the hangers so the gutter is at the proper height. Shift the hangers slightly to one side to avoid using the original nail or screw holes. Patch old nail or screw holes with gutter and lap seal or silicone caulk.

If you have to realign the entire gutter, remove it with the aid of one or two helpers. Establish a level line at the correct height on the fascia or rafter tails by taking a series of measurements with a long level or water level and marking the proper height at each end. Depending on the gutter style and mounting arrangement, the height of the line can either represent the top edge of the gutter, the locations of the screw or nail holes on the mounting brackets, or the bottom edge of the gutter. At the downspout end, measure down from your level mark to provide a slope of ¼ in. per 4 ft., and snap a chalkline between each end. NOTE: Long runs often have two gutters—one at or near each end. In in this case, find the centerpoint between both downspouts and make this the high point, sloping the gutter toward each downspout from the center. Reinstall the gutter to the chalkline, using new hangers and connectors.

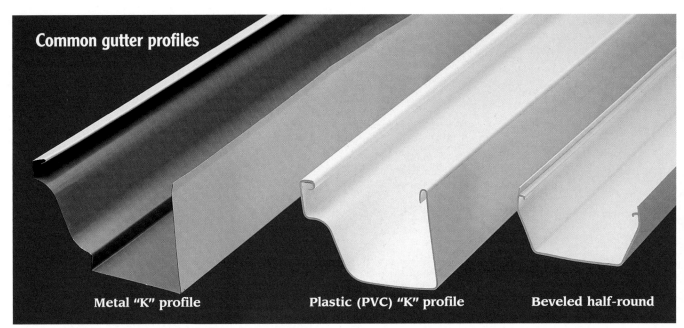

Common gutter profiles

Metal "K" profile **Plastic (PVC) "K" profile** **Beveled half-round**

Identify the profile and size of your gutter sections before purchasing replacement sections or hangers. By far the most common profile for both metal and plastic gutters is the "K" style with its ogee profile on the front edge. The 5-in. metal "K" profile and the 4½-in. plastic "K" profile shown above are the two most common versions made today. Half-round or beveled half-round versions continue to be manufactured but are more difficult to find. Over the years sizes and profiles

have varied. If your house has an older gutter system, you may have a difficult time locating replacement sections or hangers that match exactly. In the case of metal gutters, you can have new sections bent to match at a sheet metal fabricating shop, but that isn't an option with plastic gutters. If you can't find matching plastic gutter styles, your only recourse may be to replace the entire affected run, including hangers and downspouts.

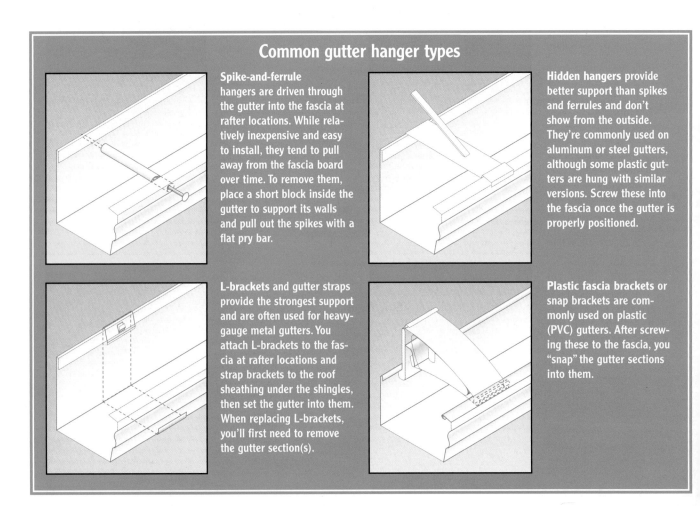

Common gutter hanger types

Spike-and-ferrule hangers are driven through the gutter into the fascia at rafter locations. While relatively inexpensive and easy to install, they tend to pull away from the fascia board over time. To remove them, place a short block inside the gutter to support its walls and pull out the spikes with a flat pry bar.

Hidden hangers provide better support than spikes and ferrules and don't show from the outside. They're commonly used on aluminum or steel gutters, although some plastic gutters are hung with similar versions. Screw these into the fascia once the gutter is properly positioned.

L-brackets and gutter straps provide the strongest support and are often used for heavy-gauge metal gutters. You attach L-brackets to the fascia at rafter locations and strap brackets to the roof sheathing under the shingles, then set the gutter into them. When replacing L-brackets, you'll first need to remove the gutter section(s).

Plastic fascia brackets or snap brackets are commonly used on plastic (PVC) gutters. After screwing these to the fascia, you "snap" the gutter sections into them.

Plastic downspouts

The downspout connectors on plastic gutter systems are potential trouble areas for developing leaks. the main cause of problems is expansion and contraction of the gutter sections, which can cause the sections to detach from the connectors. For this reason, most plastic downspouts sold today are calibrated to serve as a guide for cutting sections to the correct length. The ends of the gutter sections, when properly installed, should extend into the downspout connector up to the lines that correspond with the air temperature at the time of installation. That way, when expansion and contraction cause the gutter sections to move relative to the downspout connector, they won't move so far that the joint is compromised.

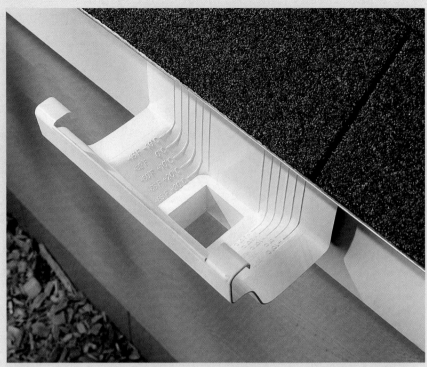

The calibration marks on plastic downspout connectors are used as guides for installing or replacing gutter sections that fit into the connectors. They refer to the air temperature at the time of installation.

Gutter lap is a specialty caulk designed for use with gutters and flashing. It is an elasticized material that will expand and contract along with the gutter sections.

Quick fixes for small leaks

Metal gutters often rust through where standing water occurs, usually as a result of a sagging section or improper slope toward the downspout. Loose joints are another cause of leaks. You can often spot leaky areas from the ground by the stains they create on the gutter or fascia behind. Areas prone to standing water or slow flow can be spotted by "tide marks" inside the gutter—mineral deposits left on the gutter walls as water evaporates.

If the inside of the gutter shows signs of rust but no holes are apparent, lightly brush the area with a wire brush (be careful not to remove the zinc coating on galvanized gutters.) Apply gutter sealant (like the gutter lap shown to the left) or roof cement to the leaky area. If the leak is on a flat surface, feather out the sealant.

How to repair a leaky joint in a metal gutter system

1 Disassemble the leaky joint by removing the connector strap (if you're careful removing it, you might be able to reuse it later). You may need to remove gutter hangers near the connectors to do this. With a wire brush, scrape old sealant off the inside surface of the connector. Also clean old sealant from the gutter sections.

2 Apply new gutter sealant to the inside surface of the connector. There should be a heavy bead on each side of the joint between gutter sections. Snap the connector back into place (do not use metal fasteners to attach the connector). Reattach any hangers you removed. For extra protection, apply gutter sealant to the joint inside the gutter and feather the sealant out to avoid creating a ridge.

How to repair a leaky joint in a plastic gutter system

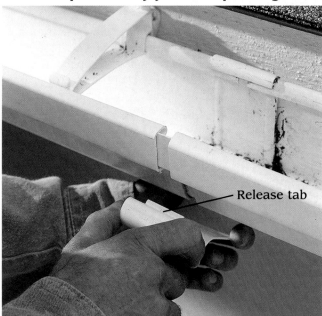

Release tab

1 If your plastic gutter system develops at leak at a connector joint, the best solution is to remove and replace the connector in the affected area. Because the expansion and contraction rates are so high with plastic, even elasticized gutter sealants tend to pull apart under stress. Examine the connector to determine how it's attached, then remove it (some, like the two-part connector above, have release tabs you pull up to detach the connector).

2 Clean the gutter sections near the joint with soap and water, then install a new connector of the same style as the one you removed. In the system shown above, the interior part of the two-part connector has a factory-applied foam sealant bead on each side. The exterior part snaps around the outside of the gutter and draws the interior portion tight against the gutter section, creating a watertight seal in conjunction with the foam sealant beads.

How to patch a damaged gutter section in a metal gutter system

1 Repair larger holes or rusted areas in metal gutters with a metal patch of the same material as the gutter. Remove rust and debris around the damaged area with a wire brush, then clean with an abrasive pad dipped in mineral spirits. Allow to dry, then spread a ⅛ in. thick bead of plastic roof cement or gutter lap over the damaged area and slightly beyond it, feathering the edges.

2 Cut a piece of metal flashing to cover the damage and bed it into the wet cement. Again, make sure the flashing is the same type of metal as the gutters.

3 Seal the edges of the patch with more cement, then feather out the edges to prevent damming.

OPTION: Use fiberglass repair fabric. Instead of using a patch cut from metal flashing, you can use fiberglass gutter repair fabric to patch metal gutters. The fabric (often sold with other products as a gutter repair kit) is also bedded into roof cement or gutter lap, then is completely covered with a smoothed and feather-out layer of cement or gutter lap. The product, similar in function to wallboard tape, is a little easier to handle than metal flashing.

How to replace a damaged gutter section

1 Mark a vertical cutting line near each end of the damaged metal gutter section. Hold the gutter firmly with one hand and start cutting the outside face of the gutter along the cutting lines, using a hacksaw. As you near the back of the gutter, either slip a thin backer board between the gutter and fascia to avoid damaging the fascia and shingles, or finish the cut with aviator snips. Remove the damaged section.

2 Cut a replacement section from gutter material that closely matches the original. The replacement section should be at least 6 in. longer than damaged section you removed. *TIP:* To brace the gutter section, making it easier to cut, slip 2×4 blocking inside the gutter. Smooth and deburr the cut ends on the new piece and the old gutter with a fine file or emery cloth. Also remove any light rust or debris from the gutter sections on either side of the repair area with a wire brush.

3 Determine the direction of water flow in the gutter. Apply gutter lap caulk to the inside surface of the original gutter on the low side of the repair area. Them apply caulk to the inside surface of the patch where it will fit over the underside of the original gutter of the high side. Slip the patch in place so it fits beneath the gutter trough on the high side and over the gutter trough on the low side. This way, water will not flow against a repair joint.

4 Reinforce the joint with three or four sheet metal screws or pop rivets (two on the front side and one or two at the back). Use stainless-steel rivets for galvanized metal gutters or aluminum rivets for aluminum. If you use screws, equip an electric drill with a 6-in. Phillips bit extension to reach screws inside the gutter.

How to repair a failed metal downspout joint

1 Metal downspouts typically are fastened together at the joints with sheet metal screws or pop rivets. If a downspout joint fails, remove the old fasteners, then disassemble the joints. Clean the downspout sections and reassemble the joint, making sure the higher downspout sections fit into the lower sections. Drill pilot holes for pop rivets or sheet metal screws through the sides of the joint.

2 Install new fasteners in the pilot holes to pin the joints together. Use aluminum pop rivets for aluminum gutter systems, and use galvanized or stainless-steel sheet metal screws for galvanized or metal gutter systems. Caulk over the heads of the fasteners with clear gutter lap or silicone caulk.

Downspout maintenance

Because downspouts are enclosed spaces, they're more likely to clog than open gutter sections. In addition to rendering the gutter system useless, the clogged downspout can cause the gutters to sag and pull away from the fascia due to the added weight of the water. You can help prevent clogging by installing a metal mesh strainer at the mouth of the downspout (See photo, right). If the downspout does form a clog, the water runoff will roll over the sides of the gutter sections and down the fascia and siding of your house. There are many tips you can use for clearing a clogged downspout, but perhaps the most effective is simply to insert your garden hose into downspout from below and work it up toward the mouth of the downspout (See

photo, far right). When you encounter resistance, turn on the water. The combined forces of the water pressure and the direct pressure from the hose nozzle will work most clogs loose. If this tactic fails, try using a plumber's snake to loosen the clog, then wash it out with the garden hose.

Repairing soffits & fascia

New fascia section

Original fascia section

Groove for soffit

"Scarf" joint

Replace damaged fascia sections with new material. Cut grooves for plywood soffits and prime the replacement boards before installing them. A beveled scarf joint creates a tight seal.

Fascia boards and soffits provide a finished appearance to the roof overhang by covering exposed rafter ends and lookouts. They also discourage birds, wasps, and other pests from nesting in the eaves or gaining access to your attic area through open vents.

Soffit system styles and roof-and-rafter construction techniques vary widely. In this chapter, we've attempted to show a useful representation of how to repair each of the most common styles of soffit. But as likely as not, you'll find the soffit system on your own home differs in some way from anything you may find here or in any other book. In such cases, simply refer to the repair sequence that most closely resembles your situation, as well as the diagrams on the following page. By studying this information, you should be able to apply the techniques shown to your situation without too much difficulty. It may help to understand that repairing damage to soffits basically boils down to removing the damaged areas or panels, finding suitable replacement material, and installing the new material.

Fascia boards are attached to the rafter ends or rafter lookout on your house. In addition to improving the appearance of the home by concealing the rafters, they normally support the front edge of the soffit system. They also support gutter systems on most homes. because they're in the middle of so much action, fascia boards tend to incur damage and rot faster than some other types of trim. Fortunately, they're easy to repair or replace.

If your house has no soffits, but you'd like to add them, consider adding an aluminum or vinyl system. These won't rot and are easy to maintain. They come with all the necessary components, including soffit vents, and instructions.

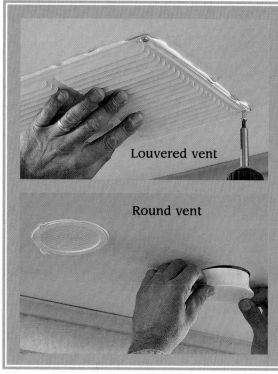

Louvered vent

Round vent

Soffit ventilation

Most soffits contain vents to allow air flow through the eaves of the house and into the attic area. The type of vent and vent cover used depends largely on the type of soffit material used. On plywood soffits (the most common type installed on homes built beginning around World War II), rectangular louvered vents with insect screening are quite common. Newer round vent covers are sized to match common hole-saw diameters, making installation easy (See pages 128 to 129).

Soffit system types

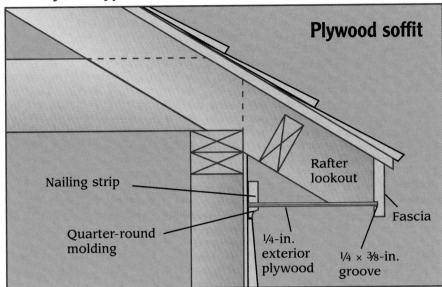

Plywood soffit

- Nailing strip
- Quarter-round molding
- ¼-in. exterior plywood
- Rafter lookout
- Fascia
- ¼ × ⅜-in. groove

Plywood soffit systems. This very common soffit system type is inexpensive and easy to install. In some cases, the inside faces of the fascia boards are cut with a ¼ × ⅜-in. deep groove near the bottom to accept the outer edges of the plywood soffit panels. The inner edges of the panels are generally attached to nailing strips mounted to the wall and quarter-round molding is attached from below to cover any gaps between the soffit and the wall. In some cases, the front edge of the soffit panel is attached to the rafter lookout, in which case quarter-round molding is usually added in front as well as in back.

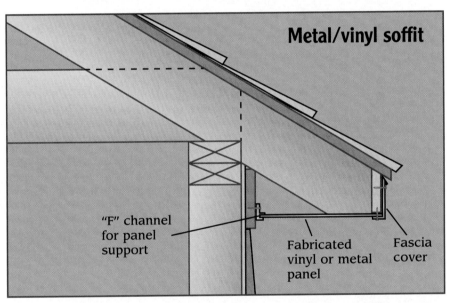

Metal/vinyl soffit

- "F" channel for panel support
- Fabricated vinyl or metal panel
- Fascia cover

Metal or vinyl soffit systems. Installed most often on homes with metal or vinyl siding, this type of soffit system is made up of interlocking fabricated panels that fit into channels in the matching molding and trim pieces (occasionally, metal or vinyl systems are installed on homes with wood or stucco siding as well). A fascia cover with a support channel on the inner face is attached to the fascia board, and an "F" style channel is attached to the wall. The soffit panels are slipped into the two channels. On some styles, each panel has integral venting, but with other types a long, continuous soffit vent is installed along with the soffit panels.

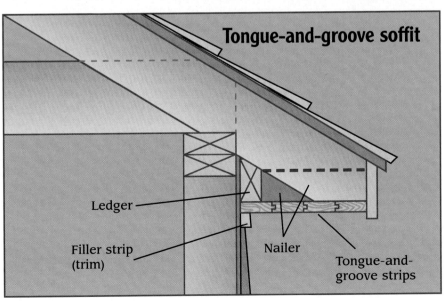

Tongue-and-groove soffit

- Ledger
- Filler strip (trim)
- Nailer
- Tongue-and-groove strips

Tongue-and-groove soffit systems. Installed mostly on older (pre-World War II) homes, the tongue-and-groove soffit system is installed using the same basic techniques used to install any tongue-and-groove materials. Unlike other types, these soffit systems feature nailers that run from the ends of the rafter to a ledger on the house to create nailing surfaces for the tongue-and-groove boards at rafter locations. Tongue-and-groove soffit systems are seldom installed today due to cost factors, as well as the fact that they're among the most difficult types to repair and maintain.

How to repair plywood soffit panels

1 Pry off any support molding or other interfering trim beneath the damaged soffit area (but leave the fascia intact). With a jig saw, cut out the damaged portion flush to the nearest rafters or lookouts on each side. If necessary, drill an entry hole for the jig saw blade. Finish the cuts flush with the rafter or lookout with a wood chisel. Remove the damaged section.

2 Attach 2×2 nailing strips to the rafters or lookouts on each side of the repair area. Use 2½-in. galvanized deck screws. The bottom edges of the nailing strips should be flush with the top surface of the plywood soffit material.

3 Cut a replacement piece from the same material (¼-in. exterior-grade plywood is most common) to fit in the opening, allowing ⅛-in. clearance on all sides for expansion. Attach with 1¼-in. galvanized deck screws, spaced 3 to 4 in. apart and driven into the nailing strips. Prime the replacement piece before installing.

4 Reattach moldings with 4d galvanized casing nails. Fill gaps and nail holes with paintable siliconized acrylic caulk and smooth with a putty knife. Reattach moldings with 4d galvanized casing nails. Touch up or paint to match.

How to repair
tongue-and-groove soffits

1 With a jig saw, cut out the damaged areas of the affected tongue-and-groove boards. Cut out all the way to the nearest rafter, lookout or nailer, but take care not to cut the board beyond the edge of the rafter, lookout or nailer. Remove the damaged sections.

2 Attach 2×2 nailers to the rafter, lookout or nailer at each end of the repair area, flush with the tops of the tongue-and-groove boards. Use 2½-in. galvanized deck screws.

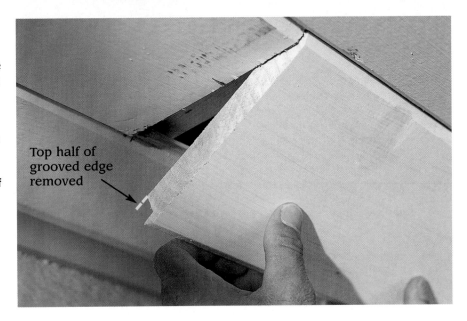

3 Cut a replacement board (or replacement boards) from matching tongue-and-groove material. You may have some difficulty finding an exact match: fir tongue-and-groove porch boards may work. If not, check local salvage yards, or find square stock that's the same dimension and cut tongue-and-groove profiles with a router or table saw, along with chamfers on the exposed edges (if the original boards are chamfered). Trim off the upper half of the grooved edge from the replacement boards, using a sharp wood chisel. Prime the board, then slip it into the repair opening so the tongue fits into the adjoining groove and the lower half of the grooved edge fits over the adjoining tongue. Attach with galvanized casing nails driven into the nailing strips, caulk the gaps and touch-up paint to match.

Top half of grooved edge removed

How to repair damaged fascia

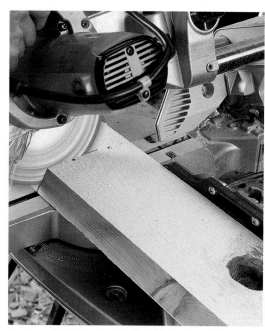

1 Remove the gutter and any shingle molding or other trim covering the fascia board. Try to keep the trim intact for reuse later. Don't remove metal drip edges or gutter flashing (but you'll need to pry it out slightly and remove nails (if present) so you can slip the fascia board out from underneath it. Pry out and remove the entire fascia board containing the damage.

2 Cut out the damaged portion at rafter or lookout locations on each side (identified by nail holes). Set your saw for a 22.5° bevel to make the cuts (the beveled ends will fit against a matching bevel or bevels on the replacement board, forming a *scarf joint*).

3 Reattach the undamaged portion of the original fascia board (the beveled end or ends should fall over rafter or lookout locations). For best weather-resistance, prime the cut end or ends first.

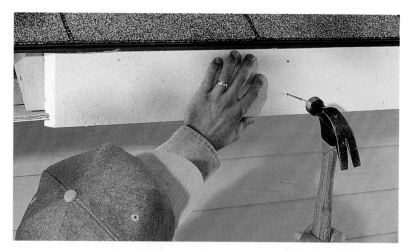

4 Cut a replacement section of fascia board from lumber the same type, width and thickness as the original fascia. The ends of the replacement board should be bevel-cut at 22.5° to fit with the original board. Prime the new piece and attach it to the rafter ends or lookouts. At scarf joint locations, nail at an angle through the joint so the nail passes through both boards (drill pilot holes first to prevent splitting). Caulk the joints and touch-up the paint.

Air movement through your attic

An attic with insufficient ventilation can be a source of problems year-round. During the summer, attic temperatures can soar to up to 150°F, adding a heavy load to air-conditioning systems. In the winter, temperature differences between the attic and heated living spaces below cause moisture to condense on the underside of the roof, lowering the R-value of insulation, rotting rafters, sheathing and soffits, and causing ice dams to form near the eaves. Ice damming, buckled shingles, damp ceiling insulation and paint peeling off soffits are all signs that the attic needs better ventilation.

Most homes employ a combination of passive vents, which include intake vents at or near the eaves and soffits, and outtake vents at gable ends or on the roof. The airflow pattern created helps equalize temperatures on both sides of the roof.

Common vent cover styles

Vent covers prevent pests from entering your home through vent openings. The most common types of vent covers include: (A) turbine-style roof outtake vent; (B) flat roof outtake vent; (C) round soffit vents; (D) louvered (rectangular) soffit intake vent; (E) gable intake vent; (F) continuous metal ridge vent (installed over shingles); (G) plastic ridge vent (shingled over); (H) continuous soffit vent.

Upgrading attic ventilation

Creating and maintaining an adequate flow of fresh air through your attic depends on two factors: having a sufficient number of air intake and outtake vents; and making sure the air passages are clear.

Intake vents: *Soffit vents* can be added to increase intake airflow on closed soffit systems. Rectangular, louvered vents are easily added to existing soffits. Continuous soffit vents provide a more even airflow but are designed to be used in conjunction with a prefabricated metal or vinyl soffit system. They can be retrofitted into plywood soffits, but the project is much more complicated than simply adding a few rectangular or round vents. Round soffit vents (also called "round breathers") match common hole saw diameters (2, 3 and 4 in.) and are thus very easy to install in soffits as well as in blocking between rafters on open-eave homes. *Eave vents* are installed in lieu of blocking between rafters on open-eave roofs, usually during new construction. Eave vents can also be installed in the house siding near the eave area. *Gable vents* are larger rectangular or triangular vents installed in the siding near the peak of a roof gable.

Outtake vents: *Flat roof vents* are simple nylon, PVC or metal vent covers that fit over holes cut into the roof, usually near the ridge. *Ridge vents* are highly effective, providing even outtake airflow along the entire ridge. Generally, they're installed during initial construction, but they can be added as a retrofit project or when reshingling the roof. *Turbine vents* are installed in

How much ventilation do you need?

To calculate your ventilating needs for an unfinished attic, first calculate the square footage (width times length) of attic floor space. As a rule of thumb, if the attic ceiling insulation includes a vapor barrier or retardant, (typically 4-mil or 6-mil polyethylene), figure 1 square ft. of net free ventilating area (NFVA) per 300 ft. of attic floor space. If there is no vapor barrier, double the NFVA figure (or 1 ft. per 150 ft). These are rough estimates only; check local building codes, as requirements may vary due to climactic conditions in your area. The NFVA of any given vent is less than it's total size, taking into account air flow restrictions by louvers and screening. To rate your existing vents, check the NFVA rating of comparable vents at a local building supplier. When buying additional vents, the NFVA rating is usually noted on the label or product catalog available at the store. Add at least as much as prescribed; even more if you live in an area with severe temperature extremes.

much the same way as flat roof vents but provide greater airflow by actively drawing air through the vent area as they spin. Even on a windless day, you'll often see them slowly whirling, due to convection currents from hot air escaping the attic. You can also purchase powered turbine vents driven by an electric motor to establish consistent air flow. As a rule, install powered vents only in roofs with a significant air-flow problem.

How to install a flat roof vent

1 Flat roof vents (also called slant-back vents) are typically placed slightly below the highest roof ridge, centered between the rafters. *TIP:* Install the vents on the backside of the roof so they can't be seen from the street. Use a minimum of two vents, positioned in from each end about ⅓ of the total ridge length. From inside the attic, mark the vent location by driving a 16d nail up through the sheathing. Center the nail between the rafters and about 2 ft. below the ridge board.

2 Locate the nail from the top side of the roof, then center the vent cover over it. Mark the outline of the base flange on the shingles with chalk or a crayon, then measure in a distance equal to the flange width on all sides and make a second set of marks. Remove the shingles within this area. Using the nail as a centerpoint, mark and cut out the roof vent hole with a jig saw and coarse wood-cutting blade.

3 Apply a coat of roof cement to the bottoms of the flanges, then slip the vent in place, centered over the cutout. Lift up the shingles and secure the vent with 4d rubber gasket nails (three nails per side). *NOTE:* Flat roof vents are unusually stamped "TOP" to help you avoid installing the vent cover upside-down.

4 Apply a bead of roof cement to the portion of the flange that will be covered by the shingles, and press the shingles into the cement. If necessary, apply more cement to seal any open joints between the shingles and vent. Wipe off squeezed-out cement with a rag soaked in mineral spirits.

How to add a retrofit ridge vent

1 Remove the ridge cap shingles using a flat pry bar. *NOTE:* Retrofitting a ridge vent is not recommended for roofs with coverings other than asphalt or fiberglass shingles, which can be cut easily with no loss of function.

2 Snap chalklines 2 in. down from each side of the peak of the roof ridge. Using a circular saw fitted with a remodeler's blade, cut along the chalklines, stopping the cuts about 1 ft. from each end of the ridge. *TIP:* Apply masking tape to the underside of the saw foot to protect it from the sharp mineral surface.

3 Remove the section of roof between the chalklines and install the continuous ridge vent product, according to the installation instructions. The model shown above is installed in short sections, beginning at the ends of the ridge and working toward the center. The ridge vent should be set back about ½ in. from the ends of the ridge.

4 Cut shingle tabs to form ridge cap shingles that span the full width of the ridge vent. Attach the shingles with roofing nails (or other fasteners if directed in the installation instructions for the ridge vent product). See page 91 for more information on installing ridge cap shingles.

How to install a gable vent

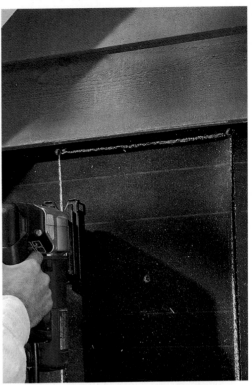

1 Gable vents are installed near the peak of a roof gable area, where they can function as both intake and outtake vents to provide airflow under gables and small, isolated roof sections. They are not designed to be the primary ventilation ports for a whole roof. Start by drilling a reference hole through the planned vent area from inside the attic. The hole should be centered between wall studs. Outline the vent opening, centering it on the reference hole. Make sure the hole is small enough that it will not extend into the nailing flange area of the vent cover. From outside, drill holes through the siding and sheathing to mark the corners of the vent opening.

2 Remove the siding in the installation area (See pages 34 to 49), then cut out the opening with a jig saw, using the corner holes as starter holes for the blade.

3 Remove the wall sheathing and install the gable vent cover using short galvanized deck screws. Because the cover will be held in place by the siding where it overlaps the flanges, it's not necessary to attach the cover at wall stud locations.

4 Reattach the siding boards, cutting them one at a time to fit up to the projected edges of the louvered section of the vent cover. After the siding is installed, caulk between the siding and the vent cover projection.

How to install rectangular soffit vents

1 Examine the eave area from inside the attic to make sure insulation or other obstructions aren't blocking airflow between the soffits and attic areas. If necessary, install plastic insulation baffles at each rafter bay (See page 131). Allow at least 2 in. of free air space between the baffles and the roof decking. Determine the cutout locations for soffit vents by driving one or more nails through the soffit (from inside the attic) to identify rafter and lookout locations. From beneath the exterior of the soffit, mark the cutout for the vent by tracing around the vent cover. Center the vents between the fascia and house wall. Draw an outline about 1 in. inside the vent cover outline to mark the actual cutting lines for the vent opening.

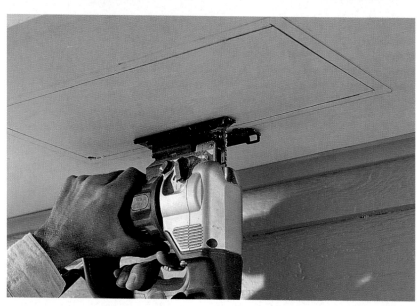

2 Cut out the vent opening with a jig saw. Drill a starter hole, if necessary, otherwise make a "plunge cut" with the saw.

3 Apply paintable caulk to the undersides of the flanges on the vent cover, then press into place. Secure it to the soffit with 3⁄8-in. rust-resistant screws.

How to install round soffit vents

1 Round soffit vents are very easy to install. Purchase the largest diameter vents you can locate at your building center (they're normally sold in 2-, 3- and 4-in. diameters). Equip a drill with a hole saw that matches the diameter of the round vents. Plot out centerpoints for the vent holes (one or two per rafter bay is generally sufficient). Try to keep the centerpoints in line. Drill holes at the centerpoints with a hole saw.

2 Apply paintable caulk around the perimeter of each round vent cover flange and press the vent covers into the vent holes. The caulk is sufficient to hold the covers in place.

Ice dams

Ice dams are a significant cause of damage to house structures and surfaces, both interior and exterior, in colder climates. In addition to creating water leaks through the roof (and the vulnerable point above exterior walls), their great weight can also cause major damage to gutters systems, sometimes even pulling them completely off of a house. The physics behind the formation of ice dams is easy to understand (See tip box, below). Basically, they're caused by poor ventilation and airflow in your eaves and attic space.

The best long-term solution is to create a "cold attic", by installing considerably more ceiling insulation and attic ventilation to prevent warm air from interior spaces building up in the attic. This tactic also works in reverse to cut down on cooling system costs during the summer months. Also, when you reshingle your roof, install fully-bonded snow and ice membrane along the eaves. Extend the membrane at least 2 ft. beyond the plane where the insides of the exterior walls meet the roof. Short-term solutions, such as pouring hot water on the ice dam or even installing heated eave cables, are largely ineffective.

A familiar sight in northern climates, ice dams are a source of great frustration for many homeowners. But by taking a few simple steps to improve attic ventilation, you can virtually eliminate them (along with the many forms of damage they are capable of causing).

How ice dams are formed

Ice dams form when heated air from the living space rises into the attic and, often in combination with radiant solar heat, melts snow on the roof. The water then runs down to the cold roof eave, where it refreezes and accumulates, building up a dam that grows larger with additional runoff. The resulting ice and water works it's way back up the roof and under the shingles and roofing felt, causing leaks near the eaves. Ice dams can also play havoc with gutters by loosening them from their brackets, deforming them or creating sags.

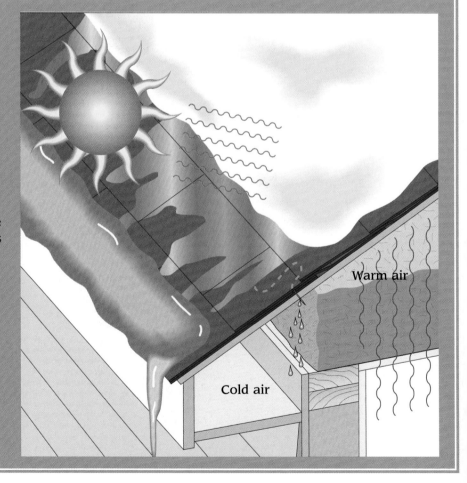

Warm air

Cold air

Installing baffles

Baffles are rigid plastic panels you install inside your attic in the eave area to prevent insulation from blocking the flow of air up through the eaves. Maintaining air flow is critical to a healthy roof system—without it, you will experience numerous problems with overheating in the summer, moisture condensation, and ice dams in the winter (in northern climates).

Installing baffles is very simple. Working as far into the eave areas as you can get, pull back the attic insulation and locate the air intake vents in your soffits or in the blocking between rafters. Make sure the vents are free of obstructions and that they are plentiful enough for your attic space (See page 124).

Insert the baffles between your rafters or trusses so the ends extend up to the exterior walls. Attach them to the roof decking by stapling through the flanges. Replace the insulation up to the baffles.

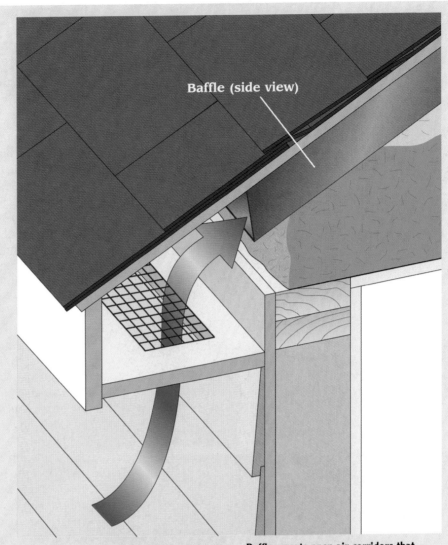

Baffle (side view)

Baffles create open air corridors that allow air flow up from the eaves or soffits and out the outtake vents in your attic roof. Without baffles, insulation can migrate into vent openings and block ventilation.

Baffles

When installing baffles around attic insulation, wear long pants, a long sleeved shirt and a particle mask. Place a piece of scrap plywood or particle board across the ceiling joists to create a safe work platform.

Weatherizing & Pestproofing

Keeping your home weathertight and pest-free is mostly a matter of diligence and, in some cases, a smart battle plan. The primary weapon in weatherizing and pestproofing is a caulk gun loaded with quality caulk. Sealing all gaps on the exterior of your home greatly reduces air transfer, while eliminating most of the entry points favored by pests to gain access into your home. Installing weatherstripping around doors and windows is another key component to sealing your home. Additional measures may need to be taken to combat specific types of pests or to seal air leaks in unique situations.

NOTE: Adequate insulation is required to minimize energy loss from your home. The scope of this book does not allow for complete descriptions on how to install insulating products. But in most cases, insulating is an easy task that can be accomplished simply by following the instructions that are provided with the product. As with weatherstripping, the most important part of the insulating process is to identify and select the most appropriate product for your situation. Check with your local building department for information on how much insulation you should have in each part of your house (the recommendations vary greatly by climate).

Weatherizing. The first step in weatherizing your house is to pinpoint the areas where energy loss occurs. General signs that you may have an energy loss problem include excessively high heating or cooling bills, excessive snowmelt or ice dams on the roof, chilly or drafty areas inside the house, and moisture condensation or frost on the interior sides of windows. To target the culprits, you'll need to do a bit of sleuthing (See *Illustration*, next page).

Pestproofing. Many of the measures that you take to weatherproof your house—weatherstripping windows and doors, caulking various cracks and crannies in siding and foundations, sealing around vents and pipes, and so on—also serve to eliminate entry points for many insect pests. Also, keeping screens in good repair will deter many flying and crawling insects (See pages 67 to 69).

Inspecting your home

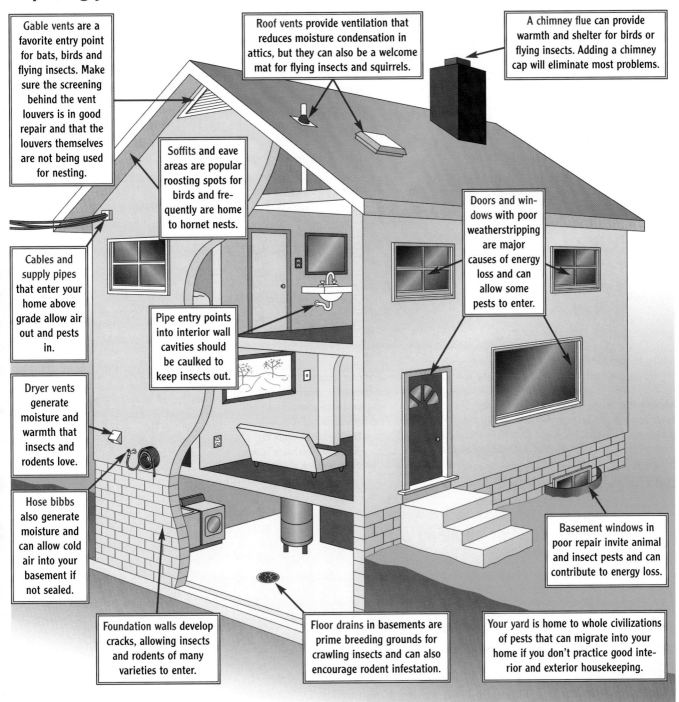

Gable vents are a favorite entry point for bats, birds and flying insects. Make sure the screening behind the vent louvers is in good repair and that the louvers themselves are not being used for nesting.

Roof vents provide ventilation that reduces moisture condensation in attics, but they can also be a welcome mat for flying insects and squirrels.

A chimney flue can provide warmth and shelter for birds or flying insects. Adding a chimney cap will eliminate most problems.

Soffits and eave areas are popular roosting spots for birds and frequently are home to hornet nests.

Doors and windows with poor weatherstripping are major causes of energy loss and can allow some pests to enter.

Cables and supply pipes that enter your home above grade allow air out and pests in.

Pipe entry points into interior wall cavities should be caulked to keep insects out.

Dryer vents generate moisture and warmth that insects and rodents love.

Hose bibbs also generate moisture and can allow cold air into your basement if not sealed.

Foundation walls develop cracks, allowing insects and rodents of many varieties to enter.

Floor drains in basements are prime breeding grounds for crawling insects and can also encourage rodent infestation.

Your yard is home to whole civilizations of pests that can migrate into your home if you don't practice good interior and exterior housekeeping.

Basement windows in poor repair invite animal and insect pests and can contribute to energy loss.

While some types of heat loss or pest infestation are painfully obvious (bats in your living areas, thick layers of frost on your windows during cold weather) others are more insidious and may require some investigation. Start by looking for clues that a problem may exist around the most common problem areas. These areas include the seals around windows and doors, foundation walls and rim-joist areas, chimneys, the eaves and soffits on your roof system and any spots where part of your home mechanical system enters the house (power or phone cables, for example).

A full inspection for weatherizing and pestproofing should take place inside as well as outside your home. Basements and attics are prime trouble areas, as are ductwork and plumbing lines. Also inspect your yard for situations that may promote pest habitation (brush piles and standing water, for example). Once you note a problem, correcting it is usually quite simple.

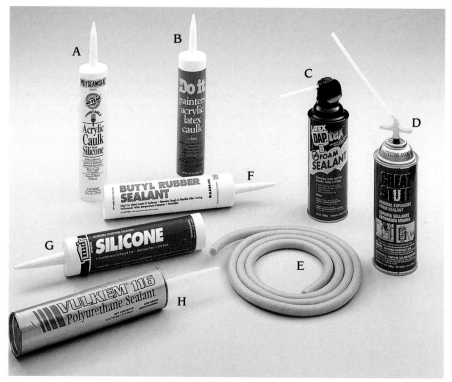

Sealants used for weatherizing and pestproofing:
(A) siliconized caulk combines the economy and workability of acrylic or latex with the elasticity and sealing power of silicone; (B) acrylic/latex caulk is a good choice for general chores because it is inexpensive, workable and easy to clean up; (C) latex-based expandable foam fills voids and gaps and is easy to clean up; (D) polyurethane-based expandable foam; (E) caulk backer rod is stuffed into large gaps before applying caulk; (F) butyl rubber-based caulk is used primarily for gaps around metal or masonry; (G) 100% silicone caulk for "invisible" caulk lines with high durability and adhesion; (H) polyurethane-based caulk has become very popular in the building trades for its durability and excellent adhesion.

Choosing caulk

Type: Acrylic or Acrylic/latex
Applications: General purpose interior caulk; can be used on exteriors, if painted.
Durability: 3 to 10 years
Elasticity: Fair
Adhesion: Fair, bonds to most surfaces.
Comments: Inexpensive, fast-drying, paintable. Use to fill small cracks and joints; do not use on moving joints. Available in colors.

Type: Siliconized acrylic
Applications: General interior and exterior uses. Adheres to most surfaces.
Durability: 5 to 10 years
Elasticity: Good
Adhesion: Good
Comments: One step up from acrylic caulks above. Reasonable price combined with relatively long life.

Type: Butyl rubber
Applications: Exterior use, good for exterior metal-to-masonry joints, gutter seams, flashings, storm windows, below-grade applications. Paintable.
Durability: 5 to 15 years
Elasticity: Fair
Adhesion: Excellent
Comments: Moderately priced, excellent water resistance, paintable. Use for narrow cracks only. Messy to work with, must be cleaned off tools and hands with mineral spirits. Takes a week to cure.

Type: 100% Silicone
Applications: Use anywhere.
Durability: 20 to 50 years
Elasticity: Excellent
Adhesion: Excellent
Comments: Popular, high-performance, versatile caulk. Generally cannot be painted. Clear types used where an "invisible" joint is desired. Moderate to expensive in cost.

Type: Polyurethane
Applications: Most interior and exterior surfaces.
Durability: 20 to 30 years
Elasticity: Excellent
Adhesion: Excellent
Comments: Super adhesion qualities, combined with good elasticity; often used as construction adhesive, especially for bonding dissimilar materials. Expensive.

Tips for applying caulk

✔ Cut the tip of the caulk tube at a slight angle, using scissors or a utility knife. The opening in the nozzle should be slightly smaller than the crack you're filling. Puncture the seal between the nozzle base and tube with a nail (insert the nail back into the nozzle when done working to prevent the caulk from drying out while it is stored).

✔ "Should I push or pull?" is perhaps the most commonly asked question concerning caulk application. While some people may have strong opinions about which works better, the real answer is that it's purely a matter of personal preference. Try it both ways and see which way works better for you.

✔ Thoroughly clean the application area and make sure it's dry before applying caulk.

✔ Spin the tail of the ratcheting plunger on your caulk gun upwards immediately after applying every caulk bead. This releases the pressure from the plunger and prevents the caulk from continuing to ooze out the nozzle.

✔ The key to achieving a good caulk bead (and it is a bit of an art form) is to maintain even pressure from the plunger and to work at a steady pace. Also, make sure the angled nozzle tip is oriented correctly, and be sure you're delivering enough material to fill the gap being caulked.

✔ If you mess up, wipe off the evidence with a rag dipped in the appropriate solvent (See the tube label) and try again.

Where to apply caulk

Exterior trim and siding. Caulk all joints around window and door frames; don't forget to caulk under win dow sills. Also caulk joints between siding and other trim strips or battens, such as corner moldings, along eaves and gable ends, and between siding and base trim. Use paintable, siliconized acrylic caulk for general caulking chores.

Entry points. Plug holes where pipes or wires enter the house. Fill large holes with expandable foam. Smaller gaps can be filled with siliconized acrylic caulk or silicone seal. When sealing around hose bibbs, squeeze tubes are usually easier to handle than caulk guns. **Caution:** Use extreme care when working around electrical service entrances. Shut off the main power supply before caulking around wires or electrical boxes.

Foundation areas. Fill gaps between the siding and foundation. Fill deep cracks with closed-cell foam backer strips or backer rope, then apply a high-grade elastomeric caulk. Also caulk between the foundation wall and the mud sill. This step is done from the inside of a crawlspace or basement. If the basement or crawlspace is heated, the caulk stops air infiltration; in unheated basements or crawlspaces, caulking is used as a waterproofing measure. Use polyurethane caulk.

Exterior wall-mounted vents. Dryer vents, exhaust vents and other wall-mounted vents should be caulked. Instead of running a bead of caulk around the outside of the vent, remove the vent, caulk around the opening in the wall, then reinstall the vent, bedding the vent into the caulk (use longer screws, if necessary). Wipe off any squeezed-out caulk with a rag.

Attic areas. Seal joints between wallboard and the top plate of the wall; extend short beads of caulk along both sides of the joist bottoms where they cross the joint. Seal joints or gaps where vent pipes, ductwork, electrical cables and recessed fixtures exit though the ceiling.

Sealing windows

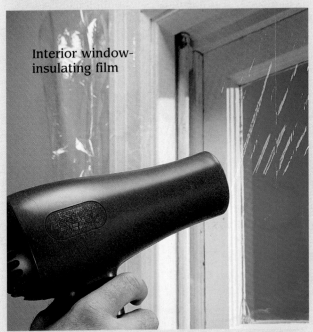

Interior window-insulating film

Exterior build-it-yourself "storm window"

Sometimes windows, especially older ones, need a little reinforcement to help keep out cold drafts in the winter. Most building centers carry a variety of clear window insulating products designed to be applied over the entire window. Some are heat-shrunk with a hair dryer to tighten the fit so they're virtually invisible. When correctly installed, these products create a vapor barrier to reduce frosting and condensation, and also create an additional dead air space on the interior side of the window to block air transfer. If visibility is not important and your storm windows are in subpar condition, staple 6-mil or thicker poly sheeting over the exterior side of the window, then tack a frame from door stop molding around the perimeter.

Weatherstripping & door sweeps (See photos, next page)

1. **Tubular gasket**

   Inexpensive and easily installed with staples, brads or self-adhesive backing strips. Widely adaptable: Can be used to completely seal double-hung and casement windows, or in tandem with other types of window and door weatherstripping. Moderate durability and visible when installed. Type shown (next page) is sponge-filled rubber. See page 139.

2. **Magnetic gasket**

   Used to seal gaps between jambs and steel doors. A rigid flange is inserted into a groove in the door stop of the jamb. When the door is closed, a magnetic strip in the gasket draws the gasket material flush against the non-hinge edge of the door. Commonly preinstalled at the factory on pre-hung steel exterior doors, can also be installed as a retrofit item. Based on the same principle as refrigerator or freezer door gaskets. See page 141.

3. **Metal-backed vinyl gasket strips**

   Inexpensive and installed with brads in same locations as tubular gasket. Like tubular gasket, metal-backed strips are also visible when installed, but are a bit more durable and have a neater finished appearance on exposed surfaces. However, they're harder to align and will kink if you over-drive the brads. See page 141.

4. **Adhesive-backed foam compression strip**

   Inexpensive, easy to install, comes in various widths, usually sold in rolls. Low durability, compared to other types. Apply only to tops and bottoms of double-hung sashes or to the insides of casement windows where the sash meets the frame. Adhesive backed foam is self-sticking and water resistant, but is often hard to remove when it wears out. Use foam strips only in places where other weatherstripping won't work—and plan on replacing them every year or two. Product shown is sold in double-wide strips that can be split along the seam for use in tight spots.

5. **Metal-backed felt gasket**

   Another fairly inexpensive product tacked to door and window stops. The felt resists damage from moving windows and doors fairly well, and is strengthened by a reinforcing metal spine that is kerfed to resist kinking. Sold in rolls and attached with brads or tacks. Felt may harden or disintegrate from prolonged exposure to moisture.

6. **Spring metal stripping**

   More expensive and difficult to install than other types, but much more durable and provides an excellent seal. Fits inside window channels or frames, making it invisible when windows are closed. Also suitable for door jambs. Available in brass, bronzed-anodized aluminum or stainless steel. Basic profiles include tension spring metal (shown in photo, next page) and V-strips. Pre-drilled guide holes for brads lessen chance of kinking during installation. See pages 138 and 141.

7. **Tack-on door sweep**

   Attached to bottom of interior door face to seal gap between door and threshold. Sweep is made of vinyl (shown in photo, next page) or polyester bristles. Bristles work well with uneven floors. See page 142.

8. **Garage door seal**

   Wide vinyl strip with profiled edges that fits into tracks on the bottom edge of a garage door.

9. **Adjustable door shoe**

   A two-part door shoe that is composed of two L-shaped members that snap together at the bottom to form a "U" shape. The female "L" is fitted with flexible vinyl strips that seal the door threshold gap. Popular for storm doors because it can be adjusted to fit doors of non-standard thickness.

10. **"Automatic" door sweep**

    A spring-loaded mechanical sweep designed to attach to the exterior side of a door. When the door is opened, the sweep lifts up to clear the threshold. When the door is closed, a pivoting mechanism contacts a strike on the door jamb or stop, causing the sweep to snap down and seal the threshold gap (See page 142). A good choice for doors with high exposure to rain or snow.

11. **Door shoe**

    A U-shaped accessory that fits over the bottom edge of a door to create a seal between the door and threshold. Most have an integral drip-edge flange on the exterior side. See page 142.

Common weatherstripping types
(See Chart, previous page)

1. Tubular gasket
(sponge-filled rubber)

2. Magnetic gasket
(jamb seal for steel doors)

3. Metal-backed
vinyl gasket strips

4. Adhesive backed foam
compression strip

5. Metal-backed
felt gasket

6. Spring metal stripping (brass)

7. Tack-on door sweep (vinyl)

8. Garage door seal

9. Adjustable door shoe
(common for storm doors)

10. "Automatic" door sweep
(two parts)

How to seal a window with spring metal

In newer homes, the window sashes and/or frames may be grooved, rabbeted or otherwise constructed to accept a specific type of weatherstripping. If the weatherstripping is damaged or worn out, replace it with the same type. Bring a sample to a home center, glass shop or other outlet to ensure an exact match.

Older windows may already be fitted with one of the universal add-on weatherstripping materials, like those shown on page 137. Or, they may not have any weatherstripping at all. Depending on the type used, you can either replace it with the same style or upgrade to a more efficient or durable style.

Testing for air leaks

To check for drafts or air leaks around windows and doors, try this trick: On a cold day, move a lighted candle or stick of incense around the interior side of the window or door (which should be closed). If the smoke is drawn quickly toward the window or door and out of the house, the weatherstripping likely needs attention.

1 Measure and cut strips to fit into the side channels for the upper and lower sash frames (four strips total). First, open the lower sash fully, then measure from the bottom of one side channel to a point 2 in. above the bottom edge of the sash. Cut four strips of spring metal to this length.

2 With the window open, install the strips in the bottom sash channels by slipping the top end up into the space between the sash and channel, with the bottom edge flush against the base of the channel. Make sure the flared side faces outward. Attach with brads (usually provided).

3 Attach spring metal strips to the top half of the upper sash channel in the same manner. Using a putty knife, carefully bend the free edges of the strips away from the sash channels slightly so they are not lying flat against the channels. Do not bend too far, and try to avoid kinking the strips.

4 Cut strips to fit on the bottom edge of the lower sash and on the top edge of the upper sash (if it is movable). Attach the strips, then attach another strip to the front of the lower rail of the upper sash (this will seal the gap between the sash frames when the window is closed).

In the situation shown on these pages, we used flat spring metal strips to seal an older wood-frame double-hung window. Before using spring metal stripping, make sure there is enough clearance between the side channels and the sashes so the window won't stick after the weatherstripping is installed. We've also included an alternative method of using tubular gaskets to seal the window. Although tubular gasket is visible, you can attach it to the outside of the window so it can't be seen from inside the house.

Most metal sliding windows have built-in weather-stripping. If you detect air leaks, remove the sash and inspect the strips. On older wood frame windows, treat bypass types as if they were double-hung windows turned on their side—weatherstrip with tubular gaskets, as shown in the sequence to the right. If only one sash moves, use a combination of vinyl strips attached to the window frame and spring metal attached to the side channel.

How to seal a window with tubular gasket

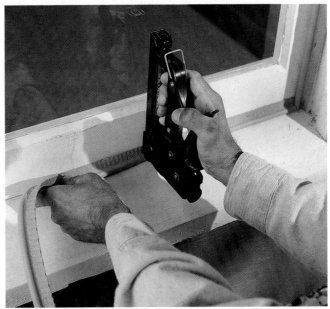

1 For both sashes, cut two strips of tubular gasket to seal the gaps between the sash frame stiles and window stops (attach the nailing flange of the gasket to the stops, not the sash). As you nail the strips, keep them slightly taut to ensure a straight, tight seal against the sash. Use 1-in. rust-resistant brads (brass or stainless steel), spaced 3 in. apart. Apply additional strips to the bottom edge of the bottom rail on the lower sash and the top edge of the top rail on the upper sash, so the window seals tightly against the sill and head jamb when closed.

Sealing casement windows

Most new wood and metal casement windows come with their own built-in weatherstripping. On older-style wood casement windows, you can use spring metal strips, tubular gaskets or metal-backed vinyl/felt strips. If using gaskets or metal-backed strips, close the window and tack the strips to the stops on all four sides to seal the crack between the stops and window sash. Attach metal spring strips to all four sides of the window frame, with the open end facing the stops. For metal-frame casement windows, apply a special grooved vinyl strip to all four sides of the frame, miter-cutting the gasket ends to fit tight at the corners (See photo, above). If the gasket material won't stay in place, run a thin bead of clear silicone seal into the gasket groove and press firmly in place.

2 Attach another strip of tubular gasket to the inside bottom edge of the bottom rail on the upper sash to seal the meeting rails. *NOTE:* metal-backed vinyl or felt strips can also be used; apply them in the same position as tubular gasket.

How to install a combination storm door

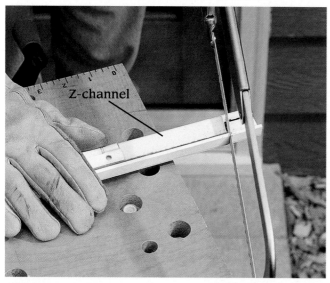

Z-channel

1 Because exterior door frames, sills and thresholds vary so greatly, prehung storm doors are sold with frame pieces that are designed to be cut down to the exact size you need. To determine the required height of the frame pieces and the angle of the threshold, measure the height of the door opening at the front edge of the door stop molding, then take another measurement where the front of the frame will be located when the frame is pressed up against the stop. Use these measurements to plot an angled cutting line on the frame pieces (called *Z-channel*) for both the hinge and latch sides. Cut the pieces to fit with a hacksaw. *NOTE:* The tops of the frame pieces should extend 1/16 to 1/8 in. above the top of the storm door.

Adding a combination storm door, or replacing a storm door that's in poor condition, will go a long way toward sealing up the entry points to your home. Although you can easily pay more for a top-of-the-line combination storm door than you'd pay for a good quality entry door, most moderately priced doors will provide an immediate payback in energy savings, and may improve the appearance of your home as well.

New combination storm doors are almost always sold "prehung", but there are a few fundamental difference in how they are installed, versus installing a pre-hung exterior door. Most notably, the "jambs" in which they are hung are actually a full-height continuous hinge that fits together with metal frame pieces on the top and latch sides. The frame pieces and hinge are attached directly to the brick molding.

Storm doors are built to match the dimensions of standard exterior doors. If your door is a standard size, you should have no problem finding a storm door for it in stock at any building center. But if your exterior door isn't standard, you'll need to custom-order a door. Custom ordered doors aren't necessarily more expensive, but plan on a waiting at least three weeks for delivery. Read the manufacturer's installation instructions carefully before beginning to install your new door.

2 Set the door into the opening so the Z-channel is pressed tightly against the inside face of the brick molding and against the edge of the door stop. Tack it in place with two or three screws driven into the guide holes in the Z-channel. Then, tack the latch-side Z-channel to the other side of the door opening and slip the top frame piece into position. Close the door and check to make sure the gaps around the door are even and the door is level. Slip thin wood shims between the Z-channel and the brick mold at screw locations, as needed, until the gaps are equal and the door is square to the door opening. Drive the remaining fasteners to attach the Z-channel frame pieces.

3 Test the door to make sure it operates smoothly and make adjustments as needed. Replace the window sashes, then Install a pneumatic door closer and adjust the tension screw so the closer pulls the door shut securely, but without slamming. Add a door swing restrictor chain at the top of the door to keep it from opening too far. Caulk the gaps between the storm door frame and the brick molding. Also, caulk any gaps between the frame and the door threshold.

Weatherstripping doors

Many of the same products used to weatherstrip windows can also be used to weatherstrip entry doors. Some types of gaskets and spring metal are sold in pre-cut sizes so you don't need to cut them to size for installation. These products are designed to be attached to (or next to) the inside edge of the door stop molding, sealing the gaps around the edges of the doors.

While obtaining a good tight seal around the door stops is very important, maintaining a good threshold seal is even more critical. A poor seal anywhere around a door will allow unwanted air transfer, but a poor threshold seal also allows pests to enter and, in extreme cases, can allow snow or rain to be blown into your home. To check the condition of threshold weatherstripping, start by looking for sunlight that shines underneath the door when it's closed. Also inspect the condition of the threshold itself, the threshold inserts (if any) and the door shoes or door sweeps. For more information on thresholds, see next page and page 72.

Spring metal strips are attached to the side and head jambs with the open end facing the door stop. Use aviator snips or a sharp utility knife to cut the strips to fit around the hinge plates and the latch strike plate. With the door closed, pry out the strips slightly with a putty knife to close up any gaps (See *Step 3*, page 138).

Steel doors: Magnetic gasket (See pages 136 to 137) can be installed into thin grooves that are cut into the edges of the door stop. A flange on the gasket is inserted into the groove to hold the gasket in place. Then, when the steel door is shut, magnetic strips embedded in the gasket snap to the edge of the steel door, closing any gaps.

Metal-backed vinyl gasket strips can be nailed to the exterior side of the door stops to seal the gaps around doors. This type of weatherstripping is easy to install and has a neat appearance. However, it is not likely to be as durable as spring metal strips (photo, top of page). Attach the strips with 3d galvanized finish nails, spaced to 8 in. apart (if the strips do not have predrilled guide holes).

Door sweeps & shoes

Door sweeps are installed on the inside of the door bottom to seal the gap between the door and threshold. The most common type is a vinyl sweep, which consists of a vinyl/aluminum strip that you screw to the door bottom. These have slotted screw holes for making minor adjustments to maintain a tight seal. This type of sweep works well only if the floor is even and the threshold extends above floor level.

Door shoes consist of an extruded aluminum channel with a vinyl bulb insert that seals against the threshold. Most styles have an integral drip cap and slotted screw holes for making minor adjustments. Because the insert is hidden safely under the door, it receives a little less wear. However, the door bottom must have enough clearance so the bulb doesn't drag against the floor or carpet when the door is opened.

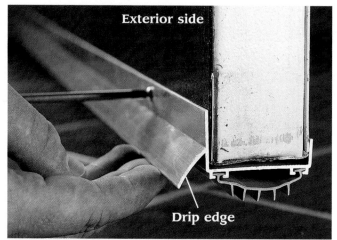

Door shoes. Attach a U-shaped door shoe to the bottoms of your exterior doors to reduce air flow and shed water away from the door. See pages 136 to 137.

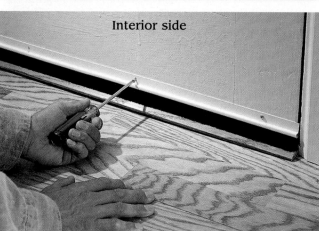

Door sweeps. These simple pieces of weatherstripping are tacked, screwed or bonded to the bottom edge of an entry door, on the interior side. They're easy to install and can be adjusted up or down slightly to fit cleanly over uneven floors. See pages 136 to 137.

Door open. When the door is open, a tempered metal spring causes the sweep to lift upward so it can pass over the threshold without catching.

Door closed. When the sweep contacts a strike on the door stop or jamb, it is forced back down to cover the threshold gap.

'Automatic' sweeps

"Automatic" sweeps consist of a spring-loaded mechanism that raises a vinyl sweep up into a metal housing when the door is open, then lowers it when the door is closed. The sweep lowers when a push rod at one end contacts a metal strike attached to the door stop. This type of sweep works well on uneven floors, or in situations where there's little clearance between the door bottom and floor. They're common on newer prehung doors, but also can be installed as an effective retrofit project. They are also the only style of sweep that can be installed on the exterior side of a door.

Pest-proofing your house

Rare is the home that doesn't suffer from an invasion of insect or animal pests at one time or another. Depending on where you live, the cast of characters and the times they visit may be different, but the challenge is always the same—how to rid your home of these uninvited guests and how to discourage them from returning.

Keeping pests out of your house is an ongoing battle that often requires the use of pesticides to provide effective control. However, this chapter focuses on non-chemical preventative measures that you can take to discourage insect and animal pests from entering your home. The use of chemical home pesticides is dangerous and can have a negative environmental impact; it should only be attempted in cooperation with a professional exterminator.

Tips for pestproofing your house

✔ Check windows and doors; screens should be in good repair and fit tightly against the window frame.

✔ Caulk joints around window and door frames; replace damaged weatherstripping as described earlier in this section.

✔ If you feed your pets outdoors, take the food and water inside at night. If you store pet food or bird feed in the garage or porch, place it in tightly sealed containers.

✔ If your house has a basement door, make sure it seals tightly—add weatherstripping if needed, and caulk all joints. Also consider replacing the existing door with a rodent-proof basement hatch.

✔ Cover open plumbing vents on the roof with insect screening or hardware cloth, secured with wire or plastic ties.

✔ Keep plants trimmed back from the side of the house, especially around the foundation. Tree branches that overhang the roof provide a natural bridge between the roof and ground for raccoons, squirrels, rats, and other climbing varmints. Trim branches at least 6 ft. back from the eaves and gable ends of the house.

✔ Inspect around roof eaves and soffits for signs of gnawing (rats, mice, squirrels), nesting sites (birds, wasps, bees) and points of entry. Caulk joints where the roof meets the wall.

✔ Uncirculating water in garden ponds, fountains, bird baths and unused swimming pools provides a breeding ground for mosquitoes and many other water-loving insects. For garden ponds, install a circulating pump and filtration system and stock it with fish to keep the larvae population down.

✔ Seal entry points from inside the house. Caulk along baseboards and around window frames. Also caulk around cabinets and other built-in fixtures to block access to hiding places for crawling insects. Caulk around pipes under kitchen and bathroom sinks and repair any leaks in drains. In the basement, caulk between the foundation wall and the mud sill.

✔ Periodically inspect inside the house for signs of insect and rodent infestation. These include rodent or insect droppings, chewed holes in food packages or contaminated stored food and gnawed holes in interior walls. Look in the attic and basement for nesting materials, webs, small holes in wood surfaces and structural members and other signs of infestation. Periodically inspect and clean underneath and behind furniture and appliances such as dressers, couches, beds, stoves, refrigerators and inside cabinets.

Remove yard debris such as brush or leaf piles, grass clippings and trash piles. Keep construction materials and wood piles away from the house to prevent infestation of termites and other wood-boring insects. Elevate lumber and firewood piles off the ground to provide air circulation (wet or moist conditions provide a breeding ground for a variety of insects). Always wear a long-sleeved shirt and heavy gloves when cleaning up yard trash or debris. Wood piles, especially, are favorite habitats for many dangerous pests.

Replace damaged screens in dryer, roof, gable and soffit vents. Add insect screening, if none exists. Caulk around all vents exiting through the roof and siding. Protective dryer vents are available to prevent insects and small rodents from entering the house. Note that if you replace coarser screening with insect screening you may need to add more vents to compensate for reduced air flow through the vents.

Tips for pestproofing your home

Seal the door threshold. Make sure the door sweep or bottom gasket fits tightly against the threshold, as this is a prime entry point for mice and crawling insects.

Install a chimney cap. Open chimneys are an open invitation to insect and rodent pests. Add a spark-arresting screen, screened chimney cap or a top-sealing chimney damper to discourage rodents and larger insects. Close the lower damper when the fireplace isn't in use.

Check the siding/foundation gap. Inspect around the house foundation for possible points of entry. Foundation cracks and gaps between the foundation and mud sill are favorite entry points for ants, spiders, cockroaches and other crawling insects. Caulk the rim seal at the top of the foundation on the interior and exterior sides. Fill large gaps between siding and foundation with closed-cell backer rope and caulk. Fill entry holes with expandable foam.

Inspect the house for leaky pipes and moist areas. Check for leaks in basement walls and damp basement floors or crawlspaces. Moist or wet areas provide good breeding conditions for many types of insects; leaky pipes or faucets provide a source of water for mice and rats. Fix plumbing leaks immediately. In kitchen and bathroom areas, keep all surfaces clean and dry; standing water in sinks, dish drainers and even damp wash rags and sponges are water sources for insects.

Identifying pest problems

Pest: Squirrels

Squirrels are one of the most aggressive animal pests. They can chew through weak parts of your home quickly. This plastic roof vent offered little resistance, and was replaced with a metal vent cover when the squirrels were not home (See page 125).

Pest: Rodents

Crumbling or cracked foundation walls are almost guaranteed to attract a host of pests, including rodents, insects and snakes (See pages 27 to 31).

Pest: Bats, squirrels

Holes gnawed in soffits create a refuge for bats, squirrels, flying insects and many other potential problems. Repair immediately (See pages 118 to 122).

Pest: Termites

Wood damage, mud channels, droppings and other waste are signs that you have a serious problem with termites or other wood-boring insects (See page 147).

Pest: Spiders

Rotten wood breeds insect infestation. Among the most dangerous are poisonous spiders, like the black widows shown here (See page 146).

Pest: Snails

Overgrown vegetation prevents shaded areas of your house from drying, which can lead to a multitude of pest problems. The snails shown here are among them. Cut back any vegetation that contacts your house.

Guide to combatting insect problems

The key to controlling all types of insect pests is to act immediately at the first sign of infestation and set up an ongoing program of preventative measures combined with effective eradication when problems do arise. Your county health department or cooperative extension agency can provide you with information on how to deal with specific pest problems.

Wood boring insects

Carpenter ants. These insects bore into moist or decayed wood to form extensive, complex galleries for nesting purposes. Unlike termites, they do not eat wood. Swarming ants may enter through open windows, vents and similar access points. Damage may appear in any part of the structure. Look for the same signs as for termite damage—droppings, discarded wings, soft or weakened structural members. Extermination methods include dusting infected areas and nests with pesticide and whole-house fumigation.

Carpenter bees. Like carpenter ants, carpenter bees bore into wood to form nesting sites. They usually enter wood from the outside of the house, boring into window and door frames, trim, and wood siding. Damage is usually localized, but can be extensive if left unchecked over a long period of time. You know when carpenter bees are present when the large, black male bees hover around your head buzzing loudly when you approach the nest. Don't worry, they don't sting. The best deterrent is to keep siding and trim painted and in good repair, and plug holes with caulk or wood filler as you find them. Household bee and wasp killers can be sprayed into the holes to kill the larvae.

Powder-post beetles. These beetles bore into unfinished, dead wood to deposit their eggs. The eggs are sometimes present in structural lumber used for new construction, or in wooden furniture brought into the house. When the larvae mature, they bore though the wood, leaving round holes. Mature beetles will also attack unfinished framing members and trim. They will not attack painted surfaces or finished furniture. Holes and small piles of droppings in exposed framing members indicate their presence. Chemical control methods are similar to those used for carpenter ants and bees. Badly damaged members should be replaced with pressure-treated wood.

Roundhead borers. These borers fall into two general types: new house borers and old house borers. Both types attack softwoods such as fir and pine. New house borers lay their eggs in the bark of weak or dying timber trees. The larvae bore holes into the wood and emerge as adults through holes in new lumber and trim within 1 year after installation; they won't reinfest the wood. Old-house borers lay their eggs in seasoned wood, thus can reinfest framing and trim members year after year, causing considerable structural damage if left unchecked. Since new house borers do not reinfest seasoned wood, the damage they do is minor and cosmetic only; simply patch the holes once the bugs emerge. Because ongoing damage from old house borers is generally widespread throughout the structure (rather than localized), whole-house fumigation is usually the only alternative to kill all of them. Consult an exterminator.

Termites. See next page.

Flying insects

Many flying insects, such as **flies, mosquitoes** and **moths** enter the house though any available opening, such as open doors and windows, open vents and the like. While most flying insects breed outdoors, they usually enter the house in search of food or water. Tightly fitting window screens and self-closing screen doors (kept in good repair) will keep most out. Eliminating sources of food and water will further discourage flying insects.

Bees, wasps, hornets, and yellow jackets. These stinging, flying insects may occasionally enter a house through an open doorway or damaged screen, but prefer to live outdoors. The best way to evict the occasional intruder is to open a door or window and wait for it to find its way out. However, these insects often build visible nests under eaves and in other protected areas on the house exterior, not to mention in attics or hollow walls. Specialized aerosol sprays enable you to zap wasps and hornets (and their nests) from a safe distance. After you've killed the insects, knock down the nest or hive with a broom or with a concentrated spray from a garden hose. To keep stinging insects from building nests in the attic, caulk or seal joints around eaves and soffits and install insect screens on open vents.

Crawling insects

Control of crawling insects (**ants, cockroaches**, etc.) consists of a combination of measures, including sealing entry points around the house, blocking access to indoor hiding places by caulking around cabinets and light fixtures, keeping food preparation areas clean, removing sources of water or moisture, and generally maintaining sanitary conditions in the home and yard. In the case of ants, trace them back to their nests and destroy the colony. As a last resort, use pesticide to control crawling insects, but use it judiciously.

Spiders. Spiders are considered beneficial because they help control flying insects in the house and yard. With the exception of the **black widows** and the **brown recluse**, most spiders in the United States pose no serious threat to humans, although their webs can be a nuisance. While many spiders can inflict a mildly venomous bite (including the unjustly feared **tarantula**), the bites are usually no more painful than a bee sting. Black widows and brown recluses typically live in dark, secluded locations, such as wood piles, and dark corners of attics, garages and basements, and usually retreat when disturbed. They bite only when accidentally touched, or trapped in clothing or bedding. If not treated promptly, black widow bites can cause serious illness or even death. The venom of a brown recluse causes a large, painful sore that is slow in healing, although the bite is rarely fatal. In both cases, if you get bit, place an ice cube on the bite and call a doctor immediately. To control all types of spiders, periodically inspect potential indoor hiding places, such as under base cabinets, furniture and storage areas. Kill or relocate individual spiders as you find them, and knock down or vacuum up the nests (black widow webs often contain roundish white egg cases that should be disposed of immediately in an outdoor trash can). Eliminate potential hiding places within and around the house by removing wood piles, trash and accumulated clutter. Caulk or seal potential entry points as you would for other pests. For widespread infestations in crawl spaces, basements or attics, treat the area with foggers or appropriate insecticide sprays, following label instructions, or call an exterminator.

Termites

Termite infestation has become a major problem nationally, causing untold millions of dollars of damage to structures every year—mostly in the South and Southwest. There are a few eradication and preventative steps a homeowner can take, but the best advice is to contact a professional at the first sign of a problem. Termites are classified into two basic groups: *Subterranean* and *Non-subterranean* (or *drywood*) termites. Subterranean termites cause more structural damage than all other wood-boring insects combined. As the name implies, these insects nest underground. To access above-ground wood portions of the structure they build mud tubes up the sides of masonry foundations, piers or plumbing pipes to bridge the gap between the soil and wood. Occasionally, the tunnels may even be freestanding from the ground to the subfloor. Common to the Southwestern United States, non-subterranean termites live in the wood itself. Damage is usually restricted to specific areas; typically window or door sills and trim, porch columns, and wood siding.

Signs of termite infestation. Look for telltale signs of termites (including discarded wings, piles of sawdust and mud tunnels) in the following areas:

• Around foundation walls and piers in crawl spaces and basements, on the inside and outside.

• Joints where poured slabs, such as patios, porches, walks or garage floors meet house walls.

• Points where decks, fences, trellises, wood sheds, porches, stair stringers, columns, and other wood structures attach to the house.

• All exposed wood components of the house, such as siding, window and door frames and sills, trim pieces, mud sills, floor joists, ceiling joists and rafters.

• Inside the house, look for discarded wings or signs of damage around baseboards. In crawlspaces and basements, look around moist or water-damaged subfloor areas, such as where drainpipes exit from toilets, sinks and bathtubs.

Preventative measures.

• Keep the area around and underneath the house

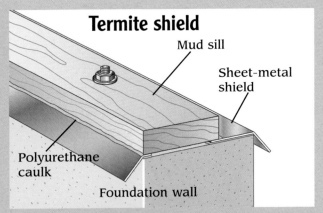

Termite shield

Mud sill

Sheet-metal shield

Polyurethane caulk

Foundation wall

Continuous termite shields are installed over the top of foundation walls before the mudsill is attached in new construction. A retrofit version of this tactic is to cut strips of aluminum or galvanized steel flashing wide enough to be inserted into the crack between the mudsill and foundation wall, and extend 2 in. beyond the outside edges of the foundation wall. Caulk the joint between the mud sill and foundation with polyurethane caulk, then slip the flashing into the joint while the caulk is still wet. Add a second bead between the flashing and mud sill. After the caulk dries, bend the projecting edge of the flashing at a downward angle. The strips prevent mud tunnels from reaching the mud sill.

free of wood scraps and debris.

• Wet or boggy soil around house foundations attracts termites. Correct the problem by fixing leaky faucets, gutters, and downspouts or regrading the ground so water runs away from the house. The soil level around the foundation should be at least 8 in. below the top of the foundation wall or mud sill.

• Caulk or patch foundation cracks, gaps around pipes and other possible entry points. Caulk the rim seal between the foundation wall and mud sill.

Professional methods. Depending on the degree of infestation, professional exterminators use various methods for termite control including treating the ground around foundations and underneath slabs (for subterranean termites), applying termiticides to infested portions of the house structure (drywood and subterranean termites) and whole-house tent fumigation.

Snakes

Despite the fear or revulsion that many people have of snakes in general, most are nonpoisonous and actually provide a service by controlling rodents (mice, gophers, moles, voles) and larger insects. However, if you live in an area where poisonous snakes are present, you don't want them taking up residence under your house or outbuildings, in woodpiles or other refuges in the yard. First, learn to distinguish poisonous

snakes from nonpoisonous ones. General control methods include blocking entry points around the house foundation and eliminating other potential hiding places around the yard. If you do run across a poisonous snake in your yard or suspect one or more are living under your house, immediately call a pest-control company to evict them. Do not try to catch or kill the snake by yourself. (If you are eco-minded, hire a pest controller who will relocate the snake to a suitable environment rather than killing it.)

Bats

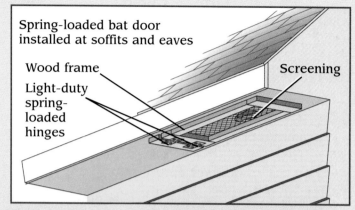

Spring-loaded bat door installed at soffits and eaves

Wood frame

Light-duty spring-loaded hinges

Screening

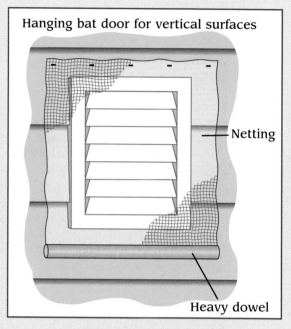

Hanging bat door for vertical surfaces

Netting

Heavy dowel

One-way bat doors are a good way to make sure the bat population has vacated your home before you close up their entry/exit point. On soffits and eaves, build a small wood-framed screen and attach it over the entry point with very light duty spring-loaded hinges. The bats will be able to push their way out, but unable to open the door and return. On horizontal surfaces, staple a heavy dowel to the bottom of a piece of netting and hang it over the entry/exit area. The bats will be able to exit, but not enter.

To keep bats out of your home, seal openings that allow them to enter, just as you would for other small animal pests. Just make sure you don't seal them inside with no means of escape. To evict them, wait until they make their nightly food run, then seal the entry point or fix the damaged vent screen. If you can't get rid of all the bats, cover their entry/exit point opening with a one-way bat door (See illustrations, above).

If a bat makes its way into the living area of your house, don't immediately make a run for your tennis racket to swat it out of the air. In some areas, bats are protected species and killing them is illegal. The best way to get rid of it (and you can bet it's as anxious to leave as you are to have it gone) is to turn out the lights and open up a door. It normally doesn't take the bat long to detect the opening and head for the door.

Animal pests

Raccoons, skunks and opossums:

All three of these relatively large critters can be a nuisance in rural and suburban areas; deprived of their natural habitat, they sometimes take up residence in basements or crawlspaces under the house. In addition to the mess they make, all three animals can carry diseases via fleas, ticks, and other parasites. Most areas have restrictions or regulations regarding the capture or killing of these animals. Check with your local department of Fish and Game or city animal control agency for control regulations. To discourage skunks, raccoons and opossums from nesting under your house or porch, keep foundation vents in good repair and block other large openings that allow access. To drive them out, place

mothballs, pans of ammonia or strong lights under the house. Remove food sources from the yard, such as pet food and water dishes, and place trash in garbage cans with securely locking lids. *Note:* Raccoons are agile climbers, and may nest in attics as well as under the house. To keep raccoons off the roof, cut back over-hanging limbs.

Squirrels:

While there are several different species across the country, squirrels fall into two main groups: tree squirrels and ground squirrels. Squirrels can do considerable damage to gardens and can transmit diseases via fleas. Tree squirrels often nest in attics, wall voids, dropped ceilings in garages and outbuildings. Ground squirrels typically live in burrows in open fields or vacant lots, although they may occasionally burrow under a deck or detached shed in the yard. Tree squirrels usually enter attics through torn vent screens and other existing openings around eaves, although they can also gnaw holes to gain access. To discourage squirrels, block entry points into the attic or other nesting area. Repair gnawed holes as soon as you find them. Wearing gloves, clean up nesting sites and wash the area with ammonia or anti-bacterial household cleaner. Trim back overhanging tree branches or install squirrel guards to tree trunks and major branches.

Birds

While most people enjoy having birds on their property, the nests they make in eaves, chimneys, ledges and other parts of the house, as well as the droppings they leave on roof peaks and window sills, can make the house look unsightly. Nuisance birds include pigeons, starlings, sparrows, swallows, and, in coastal areas, sea gulls.

To keep birds from roosting on roof peaks, parapets, chimneys, window sills and other parts of the house, try applying sticky repellent gels to these areas. Available in squeeze tubes or caulk tubes, these harmless repellents remain tacky for about one year. If problems persist, you may want to look into installing bird spikes on the problem area of your house (See photo, right). Bird spikes are thin-gauge wire fashioned into porcupine-like quills that discourage birds from roosting.

Other deterrents include scarecrows (such as plastic owls or falcons) placed on the roof or near nesting sites, sonic devices and whirligigs, although these tend to be short-term solutions because the birds soon get used to them. Plastic owls will be more effective if you relocate them every few months. Hanging aluminum pie tins, foil strips or bird netting over nesting sites will also keep birds from nesting at the same site.

Bird spikes are thin-gauge wire quills that are sold in rolls and attached to nesting or roosting areas, like ledges or eaves, to discourage birds from landing.

Mice & rats

Mice. Telltale signs of mice include small droppings inside cabinets, around sinks and under refrigerators, small gnawed holes in baseboards and door bottoms, gnawed-on food boxes and nests consisting of shredded paper or fabrics. Mice will set up nests in secluded areas such as inside wall voids, underneath base cabinets and other permanent fixtures, or in the attic or basement. Usually, the only time you'll see these nocturnal rodents is when you turn on a light at night.

Preventative measures. General preventative measures against mouse infiltration include storing grains, cereals and other dry foods in sealed metal or glass containers. Also remove sources of food and water by keeping kitchen and pantry areas clean and repairing plumbing or faucet leaks in kitchens, bathrooms, and laundry rooms. Bear in mind that, unlike other rodents, mice have collapsible skulls that enable them to squeeze through cracks as narrow as ¼ in. Patch or caulk all cracks and crannies on interior and exterior walls and baseboards and keep vent and window screens in good condition. Weatherstrip around doors and windows.

Traps and poisons. While trapping the occasional mouse is often a necessity, it's an unpleasant chore, to say the least. Poison baits are another alternative, but pose other problems, such as finding and removing the carcass once the mouse has been dispatched, and accidental poisoning of children or pets. Some new rodentcides on the market are relatively nontoxic to humans and larger animals. "Tamper-proof" bait traps are also available. If you do need to set traps or use poison baits, place them in areas that cannot be accessed by children or pets. Wear gloves when handling the dead mouse to avoid bites from fleas and other mouse parasites.

Rats. Many of the control measures taken for mice also apply to rats. Rats require larger openings to enter the house, but will readily gnaw their own to gain access. Also, rats are good swimmers, and thus can enter the house through the sewer system, exiting through open drains and toilets. Rats keep their teeth sharp by gnawing, and can cause extensive damage to household items, walls, electrical wiring and even plastic drain pipes. Like mice, rats (and their parasites) carry diseases. Two common types of rats that infest homes are the *Norway rat* (also called *sewer rats* or *wharf rats*) and *roof rats.* The former generally operate at or near ground level, while the latter take refuge in attics and other high, inaccessible places. Both types can be kept at bay by sealing entry points around the home and maintaining sanitary conditions in it (removing sources of food and water). Poison baits and large spring traps are used to eradicate them, although these wary creatures are often reluctant to take the bait.

Exterior maintenance skill: Pressure washing

Pressure-wash driveways and sidewalks **to remove stains and as a scheduled maintenance procedure. Use degreaser for oil stains.**

You can use pressure washers for general cleaning of large exterior surfaces (siding and driveways, primarily), as well as to prepare a exterior walls for painting. In both cases, the strong scouring action of a pressure washer usually eliminates the need for chemical cleaners or detergents. However, most pressure washers can be used to apply cleaners, when necessary (for example, a degreaser can be used to remove oil stains on driveways). When your house siding needs cleaning, you'll find a variety of wands, brushes and other hose-end attachments for applying different types of cleaners. While these beat doing the job with a scrub brush and bucket, there's still quite a bit of scrubbing and ladder work involved. That's why most professional house cleaners and painters use pressure washers. Also called power washers, these machines rely on a high-pressure water spray to scour away dirt, grease, grime, chalking paint and other contaminants.

As a paint preparation tool, a pressure washer will blast off loose or peeling paint; but don't try to use it as a paint removal tool: the strong jet can easily damage siding. Loose or peeling paint will still have to be scraped or sanded off. If you don't want to invest in a pressure washer, you can rent a gas-powered model at most tool rental shops.

Pressure washing equipment and supplies. **Well-equipped pressure washers have two interchangeable spray nozzles—a wide, 25° fan nozzle for general cleaning and a narrower, 15° nozzle for removing stubborn stains from hard-to-reach areas. Extension wands and brush attachments are also available. Specialized cleaners are available, but for most jobs you can also use general-purpose liquid soaps (choose a biodegradable product) or a solution of of ⅔ cup TSP or TSP substitute, 1 quart bleach and 3 quarts hot water.**

Do's and don'ts of pressure washing

✔ Do not stick your hand in front of the nozzle or point it at people. the blast is so powerful, it can literally tear the skin off your hand.

✔ Do wear safety goggles to protect your eyes from flying paint chips and debris. Also wear a raincoat—you'll be getting wet!

✔ Do not pressure-wash off a ladder—you'll need both hands to control the wand (when you turn it on, it has a hefty kickback, which can kick you off balance). Instead, use an adjustable extension wand to reach high places.

✔ Do not hold the nozzle too close to the surface or too long in one spot—the strong jet will gouge wood, dent aluminum siding, erode stucco, and blast mortar out of joints in brick walls. Likewise, do not point the wand directly at windows, for obvious reasons.

✔ Do keep the wand and water jet at least 6 ft. away from electrical wires, service boxes and entrances. A shock from service wires can be deadly.

✔ Do not use a pressure washer as a paint prep tool if the exterior paint contains lead. If your home was built before 1978, or you're not sure if the paint contains lead, have it tested. Hire a licensed abatement contractor to strip the paint and dispose of it properly.

✔ Be careful when pressure-washing hardboard siding, as it is more susceptible to water penetration than other types, and is harder to fix, should you gouge it. Also, do not use a pressure washer to wash a roof—the process is not only dangerous, but can knock loose shingles and strip the mineral coating from asphalt roofing. If your roof has a buildup of algae or moss (common in humid climates), hire a professional roof washer, who will agree to do the job with a low-pressure hose-end sprayer or similar tool.

Tips for pressure washing siding

Before you start, seal off all soffit and foundation vents, electrical outlets, and leaky doors or windows with lightweight plastic sheeting and duct tape. Cover porch lamps and similar fixtures with plastic bags sealed with duct tape. If you're using a cleaning solution, also cover large shrubs, and wet down smaller plants before you start. Lay down drop cloths to catch paint chips, if necessary.

Start washing on the shady side of the house. Use a wide, low-pressure nozzle to apply soap and a narrower one for rinsing. Position the nozzle about 3 to 4 ft. away from the surface. Move the wand in sweeping, side-to-side strokes. Apply the cleaner, working from the bottom up, finishing with the soffits and gutters.

Before the surface dries, switch to the narrower nozzle and rinse, this time from the top down. Angle the spray away from windows, doors, and other openings. Try to keep the nozzle pointed downward. Avoid blasting water directly into cracks. Scrub stubborn spots with a long-handled bristle brush, or brush attachment fitted to the washer. Use an extension wand to reach high places.

Exterior primer & paint

Choosing primer and paint for exterior touch-ups is mostly a matter of trying to match the existing painted surface. If you've saved a leftover can from the last time the house was painted, bring it to the paint store as a reference for ordering new paint (you're better off not using paint that has been sitting around for a few years). You may also be able to obtain matching paint by bringing a chip of the paint to the store for spectrographic analysis. If any bare siding is exposed, be sure to apply a stain blocking primer before painting.

Exterior maintenance skill: Touch-up painting

Most home handymen can—and often do—tackle an exterior painting job to save money, rather than hiring a pro. While the work itself is fairly straightforward, it's time consuming. Plan on enlisting at least one helper to help you do the job. While complete instructions on painting a house exterior is well beyond the scope of this book, we can offer a few tips on how to touch up a few trouble spots to get an extra year or two out of your current finish. Keep in mind, though, that localized paint failure is often a sign of moisture problems with roofs and siding, such as leaks, insufficient ventilation, faulty gutters and downspouts, poorly caulked joints around doors and windows, or lack of vapor barriers. Other problems may be due to improper surface preparation or paint application, or simply old age. When making scheduled inspections of your house, make notes of all the areas where paint is failing. Then determine the cause of the problem and correct it before proceeding with the touch-up work.

How to touch-up trim with paint

1 Scrape off any loose paint and use medium-grit sandpaper to feather the edges of the missing paint area into the surrounding painted surface. Scrub the paint repair area with a stiff-bristled brush and a TSP solution.

2 Apply a coat of primer if bare wood has been exposed, then touch up or repaint the affected area. A sash brush (above) does a good job of handling trim and tight areas. Follow the instructions on the paint can label.

How to paint a door

1 While most parts of your house exterior are painted simply by working from top to bottom, repainting a door involves a more complex sequence of steps to obtain good results. Start by removing the door, then scraping off blistered or loose paint.

2 Sand the areas where old paint has been removed to smooth them out. Feather the edges into the surrounding painted areas to create a smooth, invisible transition.

3 Thoroughly clean all door surfaces by scrubbing with a stiff bristled brush and a warm TSP solution. Rinse with clean water.

4 Make any needed repairs to the door. Old frame-and-panel doors may contain gaps at the joints where the panels fit into the frames. Neatly caulk these gaps with paintable, siliconized acrylic or latex caulk. **(Continued)**

How to paint a door (Continued)

5 Apply primer to all surfaces of the door. You can use a paint roller for the flat surfaces of the frames, but you'll need to use a small- to medium-sized brush for the panel inserts and the door edges.

6 After the primer has dried completely, use a sash brush to paint the panel inserts and the profiled areas of the frames. Avoid applying too much paint. Two thin coats always look better than one heavy coat.

7 Paint the surfaces of the panel frames (the rails and stiles of a raised panel door). Again, a roller can be used to increase speed and obtain a smooth finish. Also be sure to paint the door edges, including the bottom edge. After the door has dried completely, flip it over and paint the other side. Reinstall the door.

Keep vegetation at bay

Keep shrubs, plants, and tall grass trimmed back at least 2 ft. from the foundation and siding: plants growing against the house not only harbor insects, but also hold moisture that can cause mildew and peeling paint. In dry-summer climates, remove dry weeds and tall grass growing near the house, as they constitute a fire hazard. Likewise, prune overhanging tree branches at least 5 ft. back from the eave line. These contribute to clogged gutters and provide a convenient "ladder" for squirrels, raccoons and other animals to access the roof. Also, larger limbs can cause considerable damage to the roof and gutter system should they break off during a storm. Remove high branches (up to 4 in. diameter) with a long-handled pruning saw fitted with a lopper attachment, available at tool rental shops. To prevent the entire limb from crashing down onto the roof or gutter, cut it off in short (2- to 3-ft.) sections, starting near the roof peak and working down until you've cleared the eaves. Do not position yourself directly underneath the limb; when working off a pitched roof, install roof jacks and wear fall-arresting gear. Do not work off a ladder when using a long-handled saw, as you'll need both hands to operate it. If you can't easily access the limbs from the roof or firm ground beneath, if the limbs are over about 4 in. in dia., or if you just plain don't feel safe doing the job, hire a tree service to do it.

Home remedies for removing stains

Following is a guide to removing various types of stains from exterior surfaces, using everyday products. Always read and follow product instructions and safety precautions.

Dirt and grime: First try to remove with a strong spray of plain water from the garden hose, combined with scrub brush or stiff broom. If this doesn't work, mix dishwashing detergent or trisodium phosphate (½ cup TSP per gallon of water), and rinse thoroughly. To clean large areas (such as house siding) use a pressure washer (See page 151).

Oil and grease: Use dishwashing detergent or all-purpose household cleaner that contains ammonia. To remove oil spills or spots from concrete or asphalt driveways, try this: First sprinkle kitty litter over the stain to soak up excess oil. The following day, sweep up the cat litter and scrub the area with concrete and driveway cleaner, and rinse thoroughly. Sprinkle more cat litter over the area and grind it in with your foot. Let it sit a few days and sweep up.

Mildew: Mildew shows up as black splotches on painted and unpainted surfaces, usually in humid, shady areas. A close cousin, algae, has a greenish appearance. In both cases, you can usually remove it by scrubbing with a 50/50 solution of water and household bleach. (Wear eye protection, gloves, and long sleeves; avoid inhaling fumes). If this doesn't work, or the mildew has penetrated a painted surface, use a commercial mildew remover or an oxalic acid solution, following label instructions. To prevent future occurrences, cut back bushes or remove tree limbs that shade the area, and refinish the surface with an exterior paint or stain that contains a mildewcide.

Rust: Remove rust from metal surfaces with a wire brush or brush attachment and portable drill. For badly rusted areas, sand down to bare metal with silicon carbide "wet or dry" sandpaper. Refinish with rust-proofing primer and paint.

Graffiti (spray paint): On painted surfaces, first scrub the entire area with a concentrated solution of TSP or a TSP substitute (follow label directions). Wear heavy gloves, and rinse thoroughly. Prime the surface with a shellac-based stain-killing primer to prevent "bleed-through", then repaint. For porous masonry surfaces, such as brick, concrete block or unpainted stucco, first try scrubbing off the paint with a strong TSP solution (½ cup TSP to 1 gallon hot water) and stiff bristle brush or pressure washer, as described above. It this doesn't work, apply a heavy coat of "safe type" paint stripper, following label instructions. Rinse thoroughly.

Cleaning a chimney

As a general rule of thumb, you should inspect and clean your chimney at least once a year, or even more often if the flue tends to build up large amounts of soot and creosote. Creosote is a tarry substance that forms on the inside of flue walls, and is highly flammable. If not cleaned periodically, buildups of creosote can result in a chimney fire. Generally, the frequency depends on the type of wood-burning device you have: open fireplace, closed fireplace or wood stove, how often you burn fires and the type of wood you use. Softwoods create more creosote than hardwoods; also slow-burning fires in wood stoves or closed fireplaces build up more creosote than large, hot-burning fires in open fireplaces. Inspect your chimney from the topside, with a flashlight. If you notice a creosote or soot buildup of ⅛ in. or more on the flue walls, clean the chimney.

Once you've established a periodic cleaning schedule, stick to it. If you don't want to take on this messy job, or feel uncomfortable on the roof, hire a chimney sweep to do the work. Buy a chimney brush and extension handles to fit the length, diameter, and shape of the flue. Square and round brushes are available, with steel bristles, or less expensive "poly" (plastic) bristles. Before brushing out the chimney, open the damper fully, then mask off the fireplace opening with plastic sheeting and masking tape, or close the glass doors, if the fireplace has them. If you have a wood stove or fireplace insert, you may have to disconnect a portion of the inside flue or remove the insert from the firebox before cleaning the chimney. On the roof, insert the brush into the flue, and scrub from the top down, in overlapping strokes until your reach the bottom damper area. After cleaning the flue, remove the accumulated soot in the firebox.

Seasonal maintenance checklists

Spring

Roof systems:
- ❏ Leaks around flashing (near chimney, DWV, roof vents or valleys)
- ❏ Missing or damaged shingles or nail pop-outs
- ❏ Gutter leaks near joints; sagging or pulled-away gutter sections
- ❏ Disconnected or damaged gutter downspouts, elbows and drainpipes
- ❏ Missing or shifted splashblocks beneath downspouts

Foundations & masonry:
- ❏ Damp basement walls, where moisture is coming through block faces, joints, cracks or holes
- ❏ Damp basement floors
- ❏ Mortar missing or crumbling between bricks or stonework (chimneys, foundations, steps)
- ❏ Spalling brickwork, especially on chimneys
- ❏ Concrete driveways or walks chipped, cracked or crumbling
- ❏ Sunken sections of concrete walks and drives
- ❏ Window wells pulled away from foundation or well covers missing
- ❏ Damp, moldy or mildewed floors over crawlspaces
- ❏ Clogged window well drains

Windows & doors:
- ❏ Chipped, cracked, peeling or blistered paint
- ❏ Damaged weatherstripping, especially around door jambs, sills and thresholds
- ❏ Loose or crumbling window glazing
- ❏ Sliding windows and doors drag or run roughly along frames
- ❏ Windows do not open smoothly in their frames (sticking hardware, warped or swollen window frames)

Siding & trim:
- ❏ Cracked, crumbling or broken sections of stucco or asbestos siding
- ❏ Nail pop-outs attaching trim to house, especially around fascia and soffits

Fall

Roof systems:
- ❏ Damaged or missing shingles
- ❏ Roof vents obstructed with nests or leaves
- ❏ Condensation collecting on framing members in unfinished attics
- ❏ Attic areas with insulation missing, damaged or compressed by other objects
- ❏ Gutters and downspouts clogged with leaves; gutter sections leaking, sagging or pulled away from house
- ❏ Missing or shifted splashblocks beneath downspouts
- ❏ Bird or insect nests obstructing chimney flues

Foundations & masonry:
- ❏ Missing or deteriorated caulking around sillcocks, dryer vents, foundation vents
- ❏ Insulation missing in rim joist/mud sill/floor joist cavities
- ❏ Clogged window well drains
- ❏ Dryer vents clogged with lint

Windows & doors:
- ❏ Drafts around window sashes and sills; drafts around doors, door jambs and thresholds
- ❏ Fogging between layers of insulated glass

Siding & trim:
- ❏ Caulking damaged or missing between siding and molding around doors and windows or between siding and foundation walls

Seasonal maintenance checklists

Summer

Roof systems:
- ❑ Deteriorated, rotted or damaged sections of metal or wood fascia and soffit; nail pop-outs
- ❑ Blistered or curling shingles or nail pop-outs
- ❑ Algae growth on cedar or asphalt shingles
- ❑ Overhanging tree limbs coming in contact with roof shingles, soffit or fascia
- ❑ Corroded (rusting or pitted) metal roof flashing, DWV boots, roof vents
- ❑ Holes in roof vents caused by pest infiltration
- ❑ Bats, insects, rodents or birds nesting in attic, eaves or soffits, exhaust fan ductwork
- ❑ Excess heat accumulating in attic
- ❑ Missing or shifted gutter splashblocks beneath downspouts

Foundations & masonry:
- ❑ Sweating basement pipes; moisture on foundation walls and/or floor; efflorescence present
- ❑ Inadequate grading around foundation, especially in homes without gutters
- ❑ Water entering through or around window wells into basement
- ❑ Potholes, blistering or cracks in asphalt walks or drives
- ❑ Foundation holes or cracks through which insects or rodents are entering home
- ❑ Evidence of termite infestation (deteriorated framing, above-grade earth tunnels, droppings)
- ❑ Missing or damaged caulking between foundation and trim or brick mold
- ❑ Rotted framing members, especially beneath doors and windows with deteriorated frames or molding

Windows & doors:
- ❑ Cracked or broken glass panes
- ❑ Torn or damaged screens
- ❑ Chipped, cracked, peeling or blistered paint on doors, windows and framework
- ❑ Sticking window sashes or doors
- ❑ Rot present on jambs, sashes, sills or thresholds
- ❑ Water leaks around jambs and sills of windows, doors or garage door when it rains

Siding & trim:
- ❑ Cracked, dented, warped, rotten or loose siding sections, especially near windows, doors, soffits or gutters
- ❑ Damaged or missing siding corner pieces
- ❑ Algae growth on siding, chalking or dirty siding
- ❑ Faded stain, peeling paint or bleeding around nail heads (wood siding)
- ❑ Insect nests, especially where siding meets foundation or in dark, protected corners of eaves or soffit

Winter

Roof systems:
- ❑ Ice dams forming along eaves and overhangs, bottoms of roof valleys
- ❑ Water leaking into attic or entering rooms through the ceiling or along the tops of walls from roof ice dams
- ❑ Frost or snow obstructing DWV outlets
- ❑ Ice forming in gutters and downspouts, usually in conjunction with ice dams on roof
- ❑ Water backing up behind gutters or roof decking into soffits, attic
- ❑ Condensation and frost forming on attic framing members

Foundations & masonry:
- ❑ Spalling on the surface of concrete walks and driveways
- ❑ Frozen sillcocks and pipes that run through outside walls
- ❑ Frost-heaved sections of concrete walks, driveways, patios
- ❑ Ice build-up along driveways or walks as the result of melting ice dams on roofs or from roof gutters or mis–directed downspouts

Windows & doors:
- ❑ Rattling window sashes; drafts around sashes
- ❑ Drafts around doors and between door and threshold; frost present

Index